# SOUVENIR NATION

# SOUVENIR NATION

## See:

p. 92

p. 94

**SIR WALTER SCOTT'S**
*Lock of Hair*

**FRANKLIN D. ROOSEVELT'S**
*Birthday Cake*

p. 144

p. 48

**JOHN F. KENNEDY'S**
*Tie Clip*

p. 140

*and more!*

p. 152

Relics, Keepsakes, and Curios from the
Smithsonian's National Museum of American History

**WILLIAM L. BIRD, JR.**

★ ★ ★

SMITHSONIAN INSTITUTION, NATIONAL MUSEUM OF AMERICAN HISTORY, WASHINGTON, DC,
IN ASSOCIATION WITH PRINCETON ARCHITECTURAL PRESS, NEW YORK

Published by Princeton Architectural Press
37 East Seventh Street
New York, New York 10003
Visit our website at www.papress.com.

© 2013
The Smithsonian Institution
Printed and bound in China by 1010 Printing International
16  15  14  13    4  3  2  1    First edition

Editor: Sara E. Stemen
Designer: Elana Schlenker
Prepress: Andrea Chlad

Special thanks to: Sara Bader, Nicola Bednarek Brower, Janet Behning,
Fannie Bushin, Megan Carey, Carina Cha, Benjamin English,
Russell Fernandez, Jan Hartman, Jan Haux, Diane Levinson,
Jennifer Lippert, Jacob Moore, Katharine Myers, Margaret Rogalski,
Dan Simon, Andrew Stepanian, Elana Schlenker, Paul Wagner,
and Joseph Weston of Princeton Architectural Press
—Kevin C. Lippert, publisher

Library of Congress Cataloging-in-Publication Data
National Museum of American History (U.S.). Division of Political History.
Souvenir nation : Relics, keepsakes, and curios from
the Smithsonian's National Museum of American History /
William L. Bird, Jr.
p. cm.
The objects described and pictured here are
from the collection of the Division of Political History,
National Museum of American History, Smithsonian Institution.
Includes bibliographical references.
ISBN 978-1-61689-135-0 (hardcover : alk. paper)
1. Souvenirs (Keepsakes)—History.
2. Americana—Collectibles—History.
3. Souvenirs (Keepsakes)—Catalogs.
4. Americana—Collectibles—Catalogs.
5. Material culture—United States—Catalogs.
6. National Museum of American History (U.S.).
Division of Political History—Catalogs.
I. Bird, William L. II. Title.
E161.N38 2013

973.074'753—dc23

# CONTENTS

# PREFACE

The objects pictured and described here are from the collection of the Division of Political History, National Museum of American History, Smithsonian Institution. The museum's history collection originated in 1883, when the US government transferred historical artifacts from the US Patent Office to the new National Museum on the Mall in Washington. As the collection grew by donation, specialized collecting units were established, leaving unclaimed objects in the original history collection.

While these are typically described as relics or association objects, those that I find most interesting suggest the alternate designation of souvenir. Most are small—the kind of thing that could have been carried away in a pocket or a purse. Many are pieces—fragments, really—of much larger things of intense personal and historical interest that were held closely by their eventual donors. Despite their keepsake status, most are nondescript and would likely have been overlooked or lost if not for an accompanying note. These lucky objects arrived at the museum with their labels already written.

# THE TRIUMPHAL
# SOUVENIR

**M**any years ago, while I was working for the National Museum of American History on an exhibit about George Washington, a chance encounter with a relic sparked my curiosity about the things that people save. For this exhibit, the museum had arranged to borrow a group of Washington-related items from the Mount Vernon Ladies' Association. One of the objects that came my way was a small piece of wood pasted with a handwritten paper note. The wood and note lived in a plastic sandwich bag closed with a red seal. The inscription read:

> **Piece of the triumphal arch under which George Washington passed in Trenton, on his way to New York to be inaugurated first President of the United States. Presented by Chas. Hunt. Trenton. Oct. 1891.**

Who was Charles Hunt? A Trenton employee of the Pennsylvania Railroad. And what was happening at Trenton in October 1891? The construction of the Trenton Battle Monument commemorating the first Battle of Trenton, a 1776 Revolutionary War victory for the Americans. Aside from such questions of attribution, this inscribed wooden fragment seemed in its very existence a triumph—a triumphal souvenir.[1]

Purchased casually from a postcard rack or gift shop, the souvenirs we collect today are the material descendants of earlier objects that reveal how Americans thought about the past and how it would be saved. Like the fragment of Trenton's triumphal arch, these early souvenirs are ordinary objects of extraordinary circumstance. They may celebrate an experience, an achievement, or nothing of any obvious significance, for their only allegiance is to memory. They might be known as *relics, mementos, keepsakes,* or *curios*; each term has specific connotations. A relic, for example, may be viewed as magical or mystical, but its primary power lies in the perception that it is actual and real. A keepsake or memento usually is invested with personal, emotional qualities. The term *curio*, derived from *curiosity*, refers to a thing of inherent interest. Often featured as attractions in nineteenth-century museums, curios bridged the distinctions between education and entertainment. Whether a relic, memento, keepsake, or curio, each item acquired significance from the act of taking that made it a souvenir.[2]

The term *historical artifact* has replaced the word *relic* in today's museum nomenclature, and souvenirs are no longer taken but purchased. This long transition in curatorial thought and practice can be traced through the story of the Smithsonian's origins.

The original forebearer of today's National Museum of American History was the United States National Museum, organized under the administrative umbrella of the Smithsonian in the nineteenth century. The creation of an emergent class of American professional scientists, it was not initially known for its collection of historical relics. Even before the Smithsonian Museum was first founded in the 1850s, relics had taken a back seat to exploration expedition specimens in the collections of its predecessor, the government museum at the US Patent Office. Before they were at last packed off to the National Museum in 1883, the Patent Office's relics were displayed in the manner of a cabinet of curiosities, led by George Washington's dress uniform and household effects from his estate, Mount Vernon[3] [Fig. 1].

Heretofore, the historical past had been preserved through artwork: paintings, sculpture, monuments, medals, and coins representing heroic figures and events. Though seldom accorded the value of such fine-art pieces, the souvenir-relic sprang from the same historical impulse. By the 1920s the National Museum's Division of History included a kid glove imprinted with a likeness of the Marquis de Lafayette (see page 92);

## FIG. 1

The Patent Office's National Gallery displayed this brass, engraved clothing button made in 1789 to celebrate George Washington's inauguration. One of several "GW" designs made at the time, this button has a "linked states" pattern encircling a center inscription: "Long Live the President— GW." The button was doubly triumphant for having been lost and found near Natural Bridge, Virginia, in 1856, a fact duly noted on its museum label.

*Button found near the Natural Bridge, Va. in the year 1856. On the button is engraved "Long live the President, G.W."*

| MUSEUM NUMBER 16162 | NAME | Button | Brass |
| *5359* | PEOPLE | American | |
| ACCESSION NUMBER | LOCALITY | Natural, Bridge Va. | |
| 18152 | COLLECTOR | Patent Office | |
| ORIGINAL NUMBER | HOW ACQUIRED | Dep | |
| 281 | DATES | May. 19. 1883 | |

*Button found near Nat* *X. 11.*
*made in the time of Washington*
*President G W"*

### PRESIDENT WASHINGTON.

Brass button with inscription "Long live the Prdent, G. W." Found, in 1856, near the Natural Bridg Virginia.

*77264    75.367*

a tiny piece of the French Bastille (see page 88); a fragment of mosaic pavement from the palace of the Roman emperor Tiberius (see page 98); a white dish towel used as the flag of truce to end the American Civil War at Appomattox Court House, Virginia (see page 114); the table and chairs used while negotiating the terms of General Robert E. Lee's surrender to General Ulysses S. Grant (see page 116); and a chip of wood from a railroad tie at Promontory, Utah (see page 78). With the exception of the Lafayette glove, there was nothing remarkable about the appearance of any of them. Such things might have been lost for lack of a distinguishing mark or the explanation of an accompanying note or letter [Fig. 2].

The practice of attaching notes to souvenirs attests to the social value of objects whose chain of possession—their provenance—was all. The most celebrated nineteenth-century example of the note as affidavit is the one that Thomas Jefferson fixed to the portable desk of his own design on which he composed the Declaration of Independence. Jefferson pasted this note to the surface of his desk's writing box in 1825 before sending it off as a wedding present to his niece and her new husband [Fig. 3]. Jefferson's note explains the circumstances of the desk and imagines its future as a revolutionary relic: the desk might one day be "carried in the procession of our nation's birthday, as the relics of the Saints are in those of the Church." It is worth noting that six years earlier, Jefferson had compiled *The Life and Morals of Jesus of Nazareth*, excerpting "moral morsels" from the Gospels to make a book of teachings free of angels, saints, and miracles.[4]

While a souvenir may share the mystical value of a religious relic, its power as a historical relic accrues from the extraction of the real. The souvenir's most memorable qualities are derived from a connection with an actual person, place, or event—in short, it is an association object.[5]

The history of the preservation of George Washington's Mount Vernon is instructive in this regard. Even before the estate was open to the public, visitors pried shards and fragments from Washington's home, satisfying a demand for the actual and the real. Over time the cutting of souvenirs proved to be unsustainable, and the production

## FIG. 2

A lock of hair was given to the National Museum by President Rutherford B. Hayes in 1884.

## FIG. 3

Near the end of his life, Thomas Jefferson fixed a note to the wooden desk on which he had written the Declaration of Independence in 1776. Functioning as an affidavit, Jefferson's note stated the circumstances of the desk's design and imagined its future as a Revolutionary relic.

of renewable and inexpensive commemorative wares made especially for the tourist trade took the place of this practice. The father of his country, it turns out, was also the father of his country's souvenirs.

The traveler's description of a visit to Mount Vernon is often described as a mid-nineteenth-century genre in its own right.[6] Interlaced with themes of remembrance and decay, accounts culminated with the cutting of a souvenir from Washington's crumbling estate—there was not yet the idea of preserving it beyond the Washington family. In 1799, the estate passed to Washington's nephew Bushrod Washington, who consciously maintained Mount Vernon as a memorial to his uncle, down to a Bastille key that the Marquis de Lafayette had given to the president in 1789. In 1824 the visiting Lafayette saw the key with a carefully preserved note displayed at Mount Vernon in a small, glass wall case, which Washington had placed in the mansion's center hall. Bushrod bequeathed the estate to his own nephew, John Augustine Washington, who passed it to his son by the same name. The second John Augustine Washington managed to keep the estate through most of the 1850s by selling off tracts of its exhausted farmland. In 1852 Augustine, as he was known, entered into an exclusive agreement with James Crutchett, a Washington, DC, gaslight entrepreneur, to sell wood harvested from the estate, including the area around George Washington's mansion and tomb. Crutchett fashioned the wood into souvenirs—Mount Vernon's last cash crop (see page 62).[7]

After a protracted negotiation, John Augustine Washington signed a contract to sell the estate to the Mount Vernon Ladies' Association of the Union (MVLA) in 1858. Led by Ann Pamela Cunningham, the MVLA promoted the preservation of Mount Vernon, which was described as the "one last national place" on the eve of the American Civil War. Lovingly preserved, Mount Vernon became a popular day-trip destination for tourists arriving by steamboat and, later, by trolley from Washington, DC, and Alexandria, Virginia. A steamboat tour in 1885, for example, dropped off passengers at 11:00 a.m. and returned at 2:30 p.m., allowing three and one-half hours to view the grounds and the mansion.

Groups of up to fifty passengers arriving at Mount Vernon's Potomac River wharf were encouraged to purchase estate-made souvenirs before the trip home. Arriving in 1885, the MVLA's new superintendent, Harrison Howell Dodge, noted the extensive inventory of souvenir canes, hatchets, and gavels cut from estate wood as well as charms made from the nuts of a coffee tree said to have been planted by Lafayette—all for sale by a concessionaire, with no remuneration to the MVLA. The only income derived by the MVLA, Dodge recalled, came from a twenty-five-cent admission fee and sales of milk, plants, and flowers at the estate's greenhouse.[8] On one occasion, visitors considering the purchase of canes questioned their provenance: Were they made from estate wood? Failing to be convinced, reluctant to part with their money, or both, they returned to the boat by way of the woods, where they cut their own.[9]

The idea of the unlimited natural resource died hard in the age of tourism. By 1859 Plymouth Rock had been placed under protection—a reversal in policy from the days when a hammer had been kept at the ready for the pilgrim who had forgotten to bring one.[10]

In *The Innocents Abroad*, the ever-prescient tourist Mark Twain reported his impressions of reliquism on an 1867 trip to Egypt taken in the company of a Smithsonian curator. (Twain described the Smithsonian as "that old fossil.") Twain recalled that one of their party traveled with a hammer and attacked a pair of obelisks; he tried "to break a fragment off the upright Needle and could not do it; he tried the prostrate one and failed; he borrowed a heavy sledge hammer from a mason and failed again." At the Sphinx, Twain's party heard "the familiar clink of a hammer" and knew immediately what it meant. "One of our well-meaning reptiles—I mean relic-hunters—had crawled up there and was trying to break a 'specimen' from the face of this the most majestic creation the hand of man ever wrought." Like the others, he too failed. Twain attributed the vandal's failure to the quality of "Egyptian granite that has defied the storms and earthquakes of all time [and] has nothing to fear from the tack-hammers of ignorant excursionists—highwaymen like this specimen."[11]

Other travelers made note of the gun-toting tourists who took to "pot-shotting" capitals and friezes that "had defied the hammer-toting tourist for lack of a ladder." Estimates of the number of hopelessly defaced Continental ruins varied widely. Calling for the American government to ban the importation of relics in 1881, one correspondent claimed that the inflow of ruins had amounted to "eight hundred and thirty-three thousand tons in round numbers."[12] As late as 1911 the gathering of souvenirs was described as a "national mania," an onslaught under which the monuments of the nation and the earth were "melting away."[13]

In the United States, this underside of tourism subjected public buildings and monuments in the nation's capital to wanton chiseling. Visitors celebrating the nation's centennial at the Capitol chipped away at the Speaker's desk on the floor of the House of Representatives. Meanwhile, outside on the grounds, visitors angling for a better view of the ceremonies climbed onto the lap and head of Horatio Greenough's statue of George Washington. So great was the surrounding crowd on the occasion of Admiral Dewey's return from Manila in 1899 that portions of the secondary figures on the sides of the same monument were broken off and in danger of being taken away until the collectors were apprehended by the Capitol police. On an earlier occasion, a vandal had made off with Washington's big toe.[14]

At the White House, relic hunters cut fabric samples from curtains. A high-water mark of souvenir snatching followed an architectural renovation in 1902, when visitors to the grounds made straight for a debris pile of hand-planed lathe, ornamental plasterwork, and hand-cut nails dating to the building's construction between 1792 and 1800. At the request of the remodeling project's contractors, officials closed the construction zone to visitors, putting an end to the supply but not the demand (see page 138).[15]

The development of a mass market for manufactured souvenirs was welcomed as an alternative to the pillaging of historic sites. A history of souvenir sales along Pennsylvania Avenue in 1903 noted the existence of some thirty "remembrance shops," "souvenir stores," and "memento stands." "Forty years ago," the writer noted, "no such thing existed." Souvenir stands seemed to be near the main door of every public building in the capital. As for the merchandise, "Everything is there, from sets of sea shells with a picture of the Capitol on them to knives and cups of pot metal bearing a relief of Mount Vernon or the White House." With the exception of miniature buildings made of macerated currency by the Bureau of Engraving and Printing and color postcards of government buildings published in Detroit, nearly all of the merchandise was imported from Germany [Fig. 4].

Souvenir sellers understood the value of a stand's location in a government building. "People have strange notions about souvenirs," one vendor explained. "You may take $20 worth of trinkets from my store to the Smithsonian Institution, and their value is doubled by the transfer." The three best locations in the city were in the Capitol, the Library of Congress, and the Bureau of Engraving and Printing. These received more visitors than all other government departments combined. The Smithsonian's National Museum, the Pension Office, and the Patent Office received honorable mention "as good places." It was said that the rate of vandalism to these institutions declined in inverse proportion to the volume of souvenir sales.[16]

**FIG. 4**

Printed in Germany, this colorful embossed postcard pictured George Washington's Mount Vernon. By the end of the nineteenth century, inexpensive and easily reproducible souvenirs saved tourists the trouble of vandalizing the real thing.

As Mount Vernon evolved into a responsibly tended historical site, tourism began to be associated with dutiful preservation. At the same time, however, the relics that found their way to the Smithsonian's National Museum were not yet valued as representatives of how people saved the past before the advent of preservation and museums.

★  ★  ★

The kernel of a national historical museum grew among a nation of savers. Joseph Henry, a Princeton University physicist who became the Smithsonian's first secretary in 1846, warmed to the idea of a museum only reluctantly—and only if Congress, not the Institution itself, paid for it. Henry regarded even the collections of his scientific staff to be a troublesome drain on the resources of the Institution, underwritten by the bequest of the English natural philosopher James Smithson.

Smithson had written his famous will in relative obscurity in London in 1826. The illegitimate son of an English nobleman, Smithson came of age during a flowering of English culture that witnessed the championing of democratized education. Smithson traveled widely through Europe, though never to the United States. He died in Genoa, Italy, in 1829. Not until 1835, when his nephew died without an heir, did Smithson's bequest become available "to the United States of America, to found at Washington, under the name of the Smithsonian Institution, an establishment for the increase and diffusion of Knowledge among men." After debating the propriety of accepting his gift, Congress dispatched envoy Richard Rush to London to collect it in 1836. Rush, a diplomat who had served as both US Attorney General and Secretary of the Treasury, expedited the United States's claim through the English courts and returned home with a fortune in gold sovereigns equal to a little more than one-half million dollars. The bequest included Smithson's mineralogical cabinet, manuscript collection, library, paintings, and other personal effects. Aside from the "increase and diffusion of Knowledge," no further elaboration of Smithson's intent in endowing the institution that bears his name was ever found.[17]

The resulting 1846 congressional charter establishing the Smithsonian Institution specified the public amenities of a library and a museum. Under the charter, the Smithsonian became a quasi-official, privately endowed institution governed by a board of regents to be led by the chief justice of the United States. Members would include the vice president, followed by three US senators, three representatives, and select citizens. The board of regents determined that only the interest on the fortune's principal would be spent, which, having compounded in the years since Rush had secured it, paid for the construction of the red sandstone headquarters building known as the Smithsonian Castle.[18]

Selected as the Institution's first secretary by the board of regents, Joseph Henry downplayed the part of the congressional charter that called for a museum and a library. Henry's refusal to fulfill the terms of the charter rested upon his own interpretation of the "increase and diffusion" clause of Smithson's bequest. In Smithson's day, the phrase "increase and diffusion" had held a specific meaning for the champions of working-class education who endowed liberal organizations such as the London Mechanics' Institution and the Society for the Diffusion of Useful Knowledge. Lectures; demonstrations in workrooms outfitted with scientific apparatus; and easily available tracts and journals published in the penny press for mechanics, farmers, and shopkeepers ensured the diffusion of knowledge among those who might not otherwise attain it. These educational strategies, among others, had become part of a publicly acknowledged pattern of philanthropic endowment in London by the time that Smithson wrote his will in 1826. Henry, however, parsed Smithson's bequest into distinct functions more suited to the needs of professional scientists. The increase of knowledge would be accomplished by funding original research. Diffusion would be accomplished by its publication in books. The Smithsonian's *Contributions to Knowledge* series and the secretary's annual report to Congress established an international program for scholarly exchange. Nearly every annual report published during Henry's tenure from 1846 until his death in 1878 reflects his commitment to the Smithsonian as a body for professional scientific inquiry. To doubters Henry flatly stated that "the objectives of the Smithsonian are not educational."[19]

In 1855 Henry went so far as to fire the Institution's librarian, and in 1865 he deposited the Institution's books in the Library of Congress. Henry was not as successful in resisting pressure from Assistant Secretary Spencer Fullerton Baird and his allies on the board of regents to acquire scientific study collections, which were displayed in the Castle during its early years as the Smithsonian Museum. In 1855 Henry famously proposed that the US Government purchase the Castle and its collections, an idea that he floated before the board of regents as the suggestion of the commissioner of patents. Henry had hoped to thus be rid of both the museum and the Castle. Two years later, however, Henry suddenly reversed himself and agreed to take responsibility for the government's scientific exploration specimens, which had been thus far kept under the aegis of the US Patent Office. Explaining his decision to Smithsonian regent Asa Gray, who might be excused for wondering why Henry had reversed course, the secretary confided that he had changed his strategy, not his objective. Henry wrote, "If we can make the establishment popular I doubt not that in due time we shall be relieved from the expense, if not the care, of the museum."[20]

A collection consisting entirely of ethnographic artifacts and natural-history specimens was transferred to the Smithsonian from the Patent Office in 1858. Notably, the transfer did not include any of the historical relics that were a significant component of the Patent Office collections, such as Benjamin Franklin's printing press, George Washington's uniform, or the Declaration of Independence.

Henry did acquire the services of John Varden, a local theatrical technician and museum entrepreneur who, as the newest Smithsonian employee, began transferring the scientific-specimen collections of the Patent Office to the Castle in 1858 [Fig. 5] and soon started a museum catalog book of the collection, beginning with the ethnographic objects that had been collected by Commodore Matthew Perry in Japan in 1853 and 1854.[21]

Alternately described as a curator and a janitor, Varden was an enthusiastic collector of relics and curios who came of age in the 1810s, at the tail end of the Revolutionary War generation. From Varden's vantage point in the Castle under Secretary Henry, he almost lived to see the end of the Civil War.[22]

Varden was born in St. Andrew Holborn Parish in London, England, in 1791. He emigrated to Baltimore with his family sometime in the 1790s. He served under General Andrew Jackson in New Orleans during the War of 1812 and became an active member in Washington, DC, veterans' groups.[23] A builder by trade and gifted mechanic, he was known for his innovative theatrical stagecraft and use of animated scenic features. Varden traveled among Philadelphia, Baltimore, and Washington. On occasion he traveled down the Mississippi to winter in New Orleans, where he created productions comparable to any in the northeastern United States.

Varden's theatrical career can be traced in playbills and notices; press accounts rhapsodized about Varden's machinery and stage arrangements as "all excellent of their kind," often rivaling reviews of the leading stars of the day who were featured in his productions. In 1826, for example, Varden is listed as the chief mechanic of New Orleans's Camp Theatre. For the "spectacle play" *Cherry and the Fair Star*, Varden flooded the stage with water "across which a Greek galley fully eight feet long sailed majestically,

FIG. 5

John Varden, undated photograph. Varden enjoyed the earliest and longest museum career in Washington, DC. Varden opened his Washington Museum in 1836, but soon sold his collection to the National Institute for the Promotion of Science, whose collection occupied the National Gallery of the US Patent Office. He worked for the Smithsonian from 1858 until his death in 1865.

to the great delight of the audience." The production cost a reported three thousand dollars.[24] Varden often worked in the company of the youthful English singer Clara Fisher and the English comedian and producer Joe Cowell. Cowell habitually tore out the backs of theatrical stalls to enlarge the capacity of venues in which the wildly popular Miss Fisher performed. Their arrival in Washington, DC, in 1829 set off a scramble for seats, including a request for tickets from President John Quincy Adams.[25]

Beginning in 1827, during Varden's year-long absences from Washington, he took every opportunity to collect specimens for a museum that he hoped to open in the nation's capital. In Baltimore in 1829, he collected two ostrich eggs and the "under jaw bone" of a porpoise. Traveling down the Mississippi to New Orleans in January 1830, he collected an Indian arrowhead in St. Louis, a stone in the shape of a potato, and other curios. On his way home in April, he returned to St. Louis, where he acquired silver and copper coins.[26]

In 1835, Varden began to record his many gifts, loans, and other acquisitions in four ledgers—the earliest cataloging system for what later became the collection of United States National Museum. One can only speculate how Varden came by this system—perhaps it was based on the practices of other museums that he may have seen in his travels, for example, the Peale Museums in Philadelphia and Baltimore or the private cabinets of the American Philosophical Society in Philadelphia and the Columbian Institute for the Promotion of the Arts and Sciences in Washington, DC.[27]

By 1836 Varden had amassed enough of a collection to open a one-room museum in his Washington, DC, home, which he had rented especially for this purpose in a prominent location on Fifth Street West—opposite City Hall, next to Trinity Church. Varden invited the public to visit his display of between "four and five hundred specimens." Admission was "gratis," with "curiosities thankfully received."[28] "A Visitor" writing anonymously in the *Daily National Intelligencer* expressed "mortification" at having to report the museum's light attendance. But on balance, the reviewer praised Varden for his "taste and capacity for collecting and arranging materials.…[S]hould he succeed in establishing a permanent museum here, it will, without doubt, afford instruction to many, and amusement and gratification to all."[29]

Though he had opened a museum, Varden kept steady employment at Washington's National Theatre in a managerial capacity, advertising for carpenters to help build stage sets and designing sets for *The Polish Exile, Napoleon and How to Die for Love, The Jewess,* and the musical farce *The Turnpike Gate,* starring the irrepressible Joe Cowell.[30] In 1838 Varden expanded the Washington Museum to three rooms. Admission remained free, and Varden continued to cover expenses with theater work. The 1838–39 season found Varden back in New Orleans at the Camp Theatre for another romp with Cowell.[31] Using a style of promotion that later generations of Americans would describe as Barnumesque, Varden's friends at the *Daily National Intelligencer* spun his absence from Washington as an extraordinary collecting trip taken for the express purpose of gathering "curiosities, selected by his own hand…[and] presented to him by ladies and gentlemen of his acquaintance, as something rare, and worthy of being placed upon the tables or shelves of his museum." On his return, Varden's haul totaled "no less than two thousand objects." The report singled out for special attention "Indian curiosities," cases of "conchological beauties," and a collection of "superb winged insects from India" given to him by a friend from Tennessee, the actor John Hilson.[32]

As paying attractions, museums of that era were as competitive as they were precarious.[33] Between 1809 and 1830 the closing of museums became a regrettable feature of capital life. By Varden's own account, he determined to build a museum at the seat of government after no less than three others had failed, the result being a net loss of collections to Washington city. Though Varden did not identify them, they included a National Museum organized by a C. Boyle in 1809 (exact location and closing date now unknown); J. Griffith's Museum of Natural and Artificial Curiosities on Pennsylvania Avenue opposite the Central Market, which opened in 1823 and closed in bankruptcy in 1825; and a National Museum and Gallery of Fine Arts at the corner of Thirteenth Street and Pennsylvania Avenue, which opened in 1830 and closed without notice.[34]

In each, the pattern was the same: the museum opened with a flurry of notices and advertisements seeking subscribers of standing with collections. Having built a collection by donation in a short period of time, each museum's proprietor then declared bankruptcy and left town, taking the collection with him. In making his appeal for donations, Varden acknowledged this sad history and promised the public that the collections given to him would never leave the city.[35] They never did.

Though Varden's museum advertisements were more elevated in tone than his theatrical notices, he promoted his museum as a cultural attraction straddling the realms of education and entertainment—"a place of rational amusement." Varden's frequent advertisements in the city's papers used the keywords *curio* and *curiosity* to pique the attention of potential visitors who could be turned into paying subscribers.[36]

In January 1840 Varden moved his museum from his home on Fifth Street to Masonic Hall at Fourth and D Streets. He never again worked in the theater. Varden devoted his full energies to the museum that he now presented as a two-tiered attraction on the first and second floors of Masonic Hall. Varden covered expenses with admission fees and ten-dollar annual subscriptions from patrons including publishers Joseph Gales and William Winston Seaton, and the publisher and historian Peter Force.[37] On the first floor, for an admission of twenty-five cents, Varden presented natural-history specimens, Indian artifacts, and curios. On the second floor, for an additional twenty-five cents, Varden staged changing exhibits and gallery talks with light musical entertainment. Children were admitted to the museum with a paying adult at half price, though visitors with children appear to have been directed to the first floor. The combined adult admission of fifty cents for attractions on both floors delivered an evening's entertainment. The price was the same as that of a ticket to Washington's National Theatre, where Varden had most recently worked.[38] The new Washington Museum at Masonic Hall opened to the public February 6, 1840, with a second-floor demonstration of a "Beautiful Electric Telegraph to be seen in action for the first time in this country" and "passengers carried by Electro-Magnetism…with other highly interesting phenomenon in this science exhibited by machinery and explained by Mr. F. Coombs, to whom was awarded the first premium, at the last New York Fair, for the first Locomotive Magnetic Machine carrying passengers." The program included an evening performance by the Minstrels of the Rhine, who gave "a series of their much-admired National Vocal and Instrumental Concerts," and an exhibition of "sixty-six views of the principal American and other great cities of celebrity."[39]

Varden won an exemption from city licensing laws covering ticket-taking attractions such as theaters and circuses. The Washington Board of Common Council granted Varden's request to charge and receive payment for exhibitions without a license, which conferred upon the museum the status of a quasi-public institution.[40] Glowing press accounts lauded Varden's "indefatigable exertions" and agreed that the "institution is in some measure a public one." Varden worked diligently to cultivate that impression. One writer noted the "fine collections of minerals, coins, Indian dresses, arms, &c; and a couple of living bald eagles in fine feathery."[41] Once installed at Masonic Hall, Varden made a substantial purchase sure to draw a crowd to what was by that time a paying concern: two Egyptian mummies, which figured prominently in his promotion of the museum.[42]

In December 1840 Varden reflected upon his first year of operation at Masonic Hall. In a third-person notice placed in the *Daily National Intelligencer*, he wrote, "The Proprietor of the Washington Museum…finds that, with the present number of subscribers, the great exertion, and the most rigid economy, he has been enabled to keep the establishment open." In February, however, Varden announced what turned out be his final "Great and Combined Attraction in the Saloon of the Washington Museum…a concert and an illusionist."[43]

Varden might have made his museum a success if not for the arrival of the government's Wilkes Expedition collection of ethnographic, biological, and geological specimens at the National Gallery of the US Patent Office in April 1841. As Varden later explained, he had been well on the way toward making a living with his museum before the government and the National Institute for the Promotion of Science announced its plan to display this collection to the public in the palatial gallery of the Patent Office, as Varden put it, "free gratis for nothing."[44]

By April 1841 Masonic Hall was for rent, and Varden had entered into discussions with National Institute curator Henry L. King to sell the Washington Museum's collections, cases, and fixtures. All in all, Varden's agreement with King appears to have been a good one. By selling his collections to the National Institute for display at the National Gallery of the Patent Office, Varden kept his promise to keep all donations to his museum in the city. He would be employed as the gallery's mechanic and exhibition arranger. Secure in his future, in December he married Alice Rose Ptolma of Baltimore—not a bad rebound after shuttering his museum.[45]

Varden spent the next seventeen years tending to a hodgepodge of competing interests at the National Gallery of the Patent Office. By 1853 its collections included natural-history and ethnographic specimens collected by US Army survey parties and naval exploring expeditions; historical relics and documents transferred to the care of the commissioner of patents by the State and Treasury Departments; and gifts and purchases for the congressionally chartered National Institute, including the collections of Varden's own Washington Museum. An early gallery guide published in a city directory noted the display of the original Declaration of Independence; Benjamin Franklin's printing press; the walking stick bequeathed by Franklin to George Washington; Washington's uniform; James Smithson's mineralogical cabinet; a sarcophagus in which Andrew Jackson had refused to be buried; and "Egyptian mummies belonging to John Varden, esq."[46]

Varden thrived in his new environment, showing off the Franklin printing press to a reporter, caring for the personal effects of James Smithson for Smithsonian Secretary Joseph Henry [Fig. 6], and discussing relics with George Washington's adopted son, George Washington Parke Custis.[47] Ever the showman, Varden created new displays entitled *Hair of Presidents of the United States with other Persons of Distinction* (1853) and *Hair of the Presidents* (1855), the latter a comprehensive collection of hair locks from George Washington to Franklin Pierce (see page 130). Varden lent his presidential-hair collection and a side panel from George Washington's state coach to the Maryland Institute Mechanics' Fair at Baltimore in 1853 and again in 1855. He also exhibited this

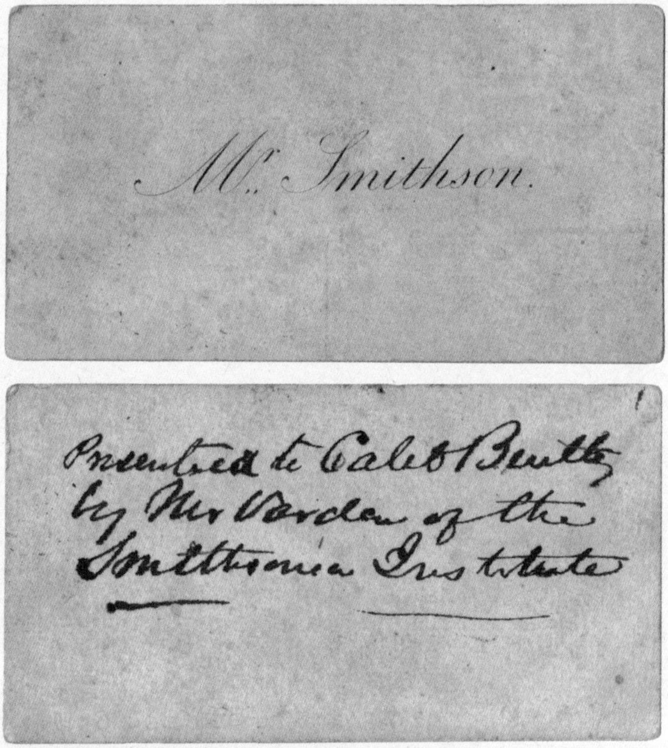

**FIG. 6**

The National Institute for the Promotion of Science acquired and displayed James Smithson's personal effects in the National Gallery of the US Patent Office beginning in 1842. There, John Varden, the collection's keeper, apparently helped himself to a lingering supply of James Smithson's calling cards. No record was made of Varden's gift when he presented one of these cards to his friend Caleb Bentley (a resident of Georgetown in the early 1790s who had made the ceremonial brass and silver plaques for the laying of cornerstones at the White House and the US Capitol); it would likely have remained so if not for the card's return to the National Museum in 1892 with an inscription on its reverse that noted its curious diversion.

**FIG. 7**

One of four side panels representing the seasons from the state coach made for President George Washington. This panel depicts spring and is encased in an oak frame. Washington used the coach to travel between the capital and Mount Vernon as well as on two presidential tours, northern and southern, in 1789 and 1791. Mrs. Mary Dunlap of Georgetown presented the panel to John Varden at the National Institute. In 1883 it was transferred with the government's relic collections from the Patent Office to the United States National Museum.

collection the same year at the Washington, DC, Mechanics' Fair held at the Smithsonian Castle, in which Varden participated as an officer of the city's Mechanics' Institute [Fig. 7].[48] The pursuit of national relics remained Varden's passion throughout his stay at the Patent Office and his later employment at the Smithsonian Museum by Secretary Henry.

In standard accounts of Varden's advancement from his Washington Museum to the Smithsonian by way of the National Institute at the Patent Office, Varden is depicted as simply having been at the right place at the right time. But Varden was uniquely qualified as a curator, with the temperament of a showman combined with the tact and discretion to build collections and make a museum. After having folded his own collection into the National Institute in 1841, Varden continued his relationships with his old donors, acquired new collections, and created special displays. When he arrived at Secretary Henry's Smithsonian in 1858, it is not clear how Varden's interest in curios may have clashed (or not) with the interests of his new employer, although collections such as *Hair of the Presidents* apparently remained behind at the Patent Office with the nation's historical relics.

A congressional appropriation to fund the museum allowed Henry the duplicitous license of enlarging scientific collections while continuing to denounce them as the ruination of the Smithsonian. Henry reiterated the Institution's noneducational objectives and added to his list of complaints the limitations of the museum's local audience. Nevertheless, the congressional appropriation that funded collection work gave the museum a modicum of legitimacy. A person now unknown painted the words *National Museum of the United States* over the entrance to the display in the Smithsonian Castle.[49]

The museum, however, had yet to acquire any national relics, and Henry remained aloof from expressions of national identity. This became a problem during the Civil War, when Henry refused to fly the American flag at the Castle. Henry reasoned that in the event of a Rebel assault on the city, the Smithsonian would be in a better position to escape destruction if it remained the extranational entity that he claimed it was, rather than the federal one its museum had become. Consequently, Henry flew no flag until he was publicly reprimanded during the celebration at the war's end. Afterwards

Henry consented to fly a flag over his family's personal quarters at the Castle, still maintaining the Institution's independence.[50]

Henry remained reluctant to take possession of the government's historical relics. These again went begging with the expiration of the National Institute's congressional charter in 1862, which left its collections in place at the Patent Office. Varden then took an active interest in the disposition of the Patent Office relics, apprising Assistant Secretary Spencer Fullerton Baird that Henry had received a letter from the commissioner of patents asking that someone from the Smithsonian take responsibility for "the large number of valuable curiosities which are being much injured here."[51]

A museum visitor had a better chance of encountering the nation's relics at one of the sanitary fairs that were popular during the Civil War. These fund-raising events were so named because they were organized by the United States Sanitary Commission, a private relief agency not unlike today's Red Cross that was charged with the care of soldiers. Held in Philadelphia, New York, and Chicago with increasing reach and cultural effect through the mid-1860s, the fairs auctioned contributed goods and services to bidders in an atmosphere of patriotic sacrifice and service.[52]

The most elaborately staged fairs presented loan exhibitions of fine art, arms, and relics. The Patent Office lent its relics to the New York Metropolitan Fair in April 1864. The fair's Department of Arms and Trophies (otherwise known as the Relic Room) exhibited George Washington's uniform, his sword, and his Franklin cane. The picture gallery featured another Patent Office loan, Charles Willson Peale's portrait of Washington.[53]

It was just as well that the bulk of the Patent Office's historical relics did not come to the Castle with the transfer of the government's scientific collections in 1858. On the afternoon of January 24, 1865, a fire at the Castle consumed the building's central tower, including the Regent's Room and James Smithson's personal papers, books, and mineralogical cabinet—relics that John Varden had looked after since the early 1840s. The fire also destroyed Joseph Henry's office, his secretarial papers, and most of the Institution's manuscript records. Eighteen days later, on February 10, Varden died. He had been home sick during the fire, and his return to the Castle the day after was said to have hastened his demise.[54] Henry's congressional report on the fire's origin identified no culprit by name, but mentioned laborers working in the Castle's second-floor picture gallery who had set up a temporary coal stove to warm themselves while reinstalling Indian portraits. The workers had mistakenly installed the stove's flue pipe into a wall that vented into the insulated air space under the roof, with disastrous results.[55]

After Varden's death, Henry tied up loose ends in Varden's first-floor Castle workroom, which had remained relatively unscathed. The contents included relics that Varden had considered to be his own. Henry suggested to Varden's widow, Alice, that her late husband's material, including coins and "specimens of natural history," be added to the public sale that she was rumored to be having. The coins alone, Henry wrote, "would bring a good price at the auction room on an evening sale." Eventually Mrs. Varden's attorney settled for the Institution's purchase of the workroom's contents for fifty dollars, with the understanding that anything not needed would be cheerfully placed at the disposal of Mrs. Varden. In due course, Henry returned two boxes to Mrs. Varden of material described as "simply curiosities and not objects of scientific interest." Henry suggested that she contact the director of a museum planned for Alexandria, Virginia, who might be interested in the material.[56] What, if anything, came of Henry's suggestion is not known.

Certain of Varden's curiosities did come to the Smithsonian, including his framed *Hair of the Presidents*, along with coins, medals, natural-history and ethnographic specimens, and the catalog ledgers of his Washington Museum, which had passed into the collection of the National Institute and through the Patent Office to the Smithsonian. Today's curators use them to document the beginning of their collections in the Department of Anthropology, the Division of Political History, the Division of Graphic Arts, the National Numismatic Collection, and the National Gallery of Art.[57]

Secretary Henry noted Varden's passing in a daybook. Though Henry did not attend Varden's funeral, he did take time to comment on Varden's theatrical career. Earlier in life, Henry himself had toyed with the idea of becoming an actor.[58] Perhaps a love of the theater was the only thing that he and Varden had in common. Varden's theatrical instincts made him a very different character from Henry, who ended his career barking about the Smithsonian's noneducational objectives, sitting in tight control over a national museum without a national identity, just popular enough to give away.

★ ★ ★

The second generation of Smithsonian scientists who led the United States National Museum into the twentieth century appreciated its collections in ways that Henry had not. They valued relics that enhanced the museum's identity as the custodian of the nation's historical past. Were they as enthralled with relic collections as Varden had been? Was history a science? Could a relic be a specimen? What did they collect?

During Henry's long tenure, the idea of a national museum had been nurtured and kept alive by Assistant Secretary Spencer Fullerton Baird, a naturalist hired by Henry in 1850. Baird arrived from Dickinson College with two boxcarloads of artifacts, including a collection of bird skins.[59] More than anyone in Henry's circle, Baird promoted the idea that collections were sources of knowledge. Upon Henry's death, the Smithsonian Board of Regents elected Baird as the Institution's second secretary. Among Baird's reliquarian passions was a lifetime collection of eighteen hundred foreign and American postage stamps. His wife, Mary Helen Churchill Baird, donated the collection to the museum after his death in 1887. Mary Baird's mother, Lucy Hunter Churchill, appears to have been a keen judge of executive ability and a battle buff, too. An acquaintance who knew of her fascination with Napoleon I gave her two of the emperor's monogrammed linen table napkins. One found its way to the museum as the bequest of her granddaughter Lucy Hunter Baird in 1914 (see page 90).

The planning of the nation's centennial celebration in Philadelphia in 1876 was Baird's main chance as a museum builder. The exhibits for the centennial fair's Government

Building were the responsibility of the Smithsonian, and the organization of these exhibits along scientific lines became the job of Baird's young assistant, George Brown Goode. A twenty-five-year-old ichthyologist from Wesleyan College when he started work for Baird, Goode went on to become curator and later the assistant secretary of the Smithsonian Institution and director of the United States National Museum. Among Goode's personal interests as a collector was a voluminous autograph collection cannibalized from his office's incoming correspondence. The collection, like Goode's career, spanned the scientific and museum worlds, from the late Joseph Henry to showman and circus founder P. T. Barnum.

Goode also saved tickets to the world's fairs and expositions for which he provided a taxonomy—a detailed classification system that, as Goode explained, sought "a place for every object in existence which it is possible to describe, or which may be designated by a name." Goode developed taxonomies for every world's fair and exposition in which the US government participated from the centennial celebration to the World's Columbian Exposition of 1893.[60]

In practice, the taxonomies that Goode developed and applied grew from the classification of ethnographic specimens and natural resources and had little to do with history. As one of four exhibits mounted in the centennial fair's Government Building, the Smithsonian contribution featured displays about animals, commercial fisheries, minerals, and Indian artifacts. Elsewhere in the Government Building were displays by the War Department, the Treasury, and the Patent Office, the latter exhibiting some five thousand patent models with a small collection of its famous historical relics, including George Washington's dress uniform, camp chest, and the Franklin cane [Fig. 8].[61]

In 1878, the year of Joseph Henry's death, Congress authorized the construction of a new museum building on the Mall to house the remnants of the government's centennial exhibits. Erected a few steps southeast of the Castle, the United States National Museum building (today the Arts and Industries Building) opened to the public in 1881. Goode designed its interior as it was being built.[62]

**FIG. 8**

This group of George Washington
relics was displayed at the 1876
centennial celebration in Philadelphia.
This display included (from left to
right) a leather bag containing
Washington's Revolutionary War
field tent, a pair of pistols, the Franklin
cane, a camp chest, a dress uniform,
a dress sword in a leather scabbard,
a dispatch case (displayed on a prop
armored chest), camp pots and pans with
a trivet, plates from the camp chest,
and a bellows. Washington's surveyor's
compass is seen on a prop side chair
that had no Washington association
but was borrowed for the display.

Goode's decision to concentrate historical relics in the museum's North Hall (where visitors entered from the Mall) raised the prominence of the collections exhibited there above the natural-history and ethnographic specimens displayed elsewhere in the balconies, connecting ranges, and three adjacent major halls. The North Hall display became more imposing with the acquisition of the Patent Office's historical relics in 1883. The transfer was accomplished by A. Howard Clark, a Wesleyan University classmate of Goode's who had joined the museum in 1881. Clark headed up the museum's Section of Historical Relics, a new subsection of the Division of Ethnology, under the Department of Anthropology, as prescribed by Goode's taxonomy. The new museum's holdings included Benjamin Franklin's printing press and a collection of George Washington's household furnishings, which Congress had purchased from the Lewis family of Clark County, Virginia, in 1878. This collection had been stored in crates in the basement of the Patent Office. Brought to light in the North Hall of the museum, the Lewis collection enlarged the museum's George Washington holdings to eight exhibit cases and became the most popular feature in the museum's most visited hall.[63]

Coupled with modern display techniques for the use of lighting and glass, Goode's taxonomy rested upon a logical sequence of display and well-written label copy. Goode favorably compared his system to that of a library, although his museum would accommodate many more visitors. The metaphor was a poor one, for his taxonomy did not account for history the way a library's cataloging system would. Rather than treating history as its own category, Goode's system placed the Section of Historical Relics under the rubric of anthropology. A table was a table, not George Washington's table, according to the Division of Ethnology. The museum visitor might be excused for ignoring the arcane rigor of such an administrative distinction. But visitors could hardly ignore how Goode's system illustrated the progress of humanity, writ large in sequential displays of hand tools, manufactured goods, and ethnographic specimens. The relationship of the museum's scientific specimens to the nation's historical relics was made explicit in the organization of the North Hall, where the story of the progress of man culminated in the history of the United States [Fig. 9].[64]

## FIG. 9

North Hall, Arts and Industries Building, about 1920. Opened in 1881, the United States National Museum offered commodious display space in a cross-shaped design of four main exhibit halls with connecting ranges and balconies. When a new National Museum building for scientific collections opened across the Mall from the Castle in 1910, the former National Museum building was designated "Arts and Industries."

## FIG. 10

Celluloid and metal buttons promoting presidential candidates William McKinley and William Jennings Bryan, collected by museum aide Paul Beckwith, 1896.

Having consolidated the nation's historical relics in the North Hall, Goode and Clark seem to have relaxed. The period from 1884 to 1890 shows the arrival of but a few donations to the Section of Historical Relics. Objects that came in during this period spoke of a working familiarity with the ways of the museum and the personal nature of collecting. The museum received its first donation of political campaign material in 1884, a box of torches and oilcloth parade clothing solicited from the Unexcelled Fireworks Company of New York. Clark's aide, Paul Edmond Beckwith, collected presidential-campaign memorabilia that could have been purchased at any city souvenir stand. The accessions included presidential playing cards, pin-back buttons, and other campaign novelties that Beckwith catalogued as gifts from himself.[65] [Fig. 10] Though the museum entertained contributions from donors who understood its goals for collecting, it made little effort to seek contributions from the general public.

In the last decade of the nineteenth century, America's veneration of its past was compounded by a search for stability in a world challenged by the onrush of ethnic immigration. The rise of ancestor worship is evident in the emergence of national historical and patriotic societies that demanded genealogical documentation from their members (among whom numbered Goode, Clark, and Beckwith) in order to prove their descent from colonial Americans. In defining objects as "American," a museum could endow historical relics with a special authority that equated possession with hereditary superiority.[66]

After 1890 Goode appears to have begun actively courting collectors of historical relics. The museum made arrangements with the American Historical Association (AHA) and national patriotic societies including the Sons of the American Revolution (SAR), the Daughters of the American Revolution (DAR), and the Colonial Dames of America. Even though Goode's taxonomy failed to account for history other than as a subsection of anthropology, it was nevertheless accepted by the American historical profession. The leadership of the AHA, after all, was drawn from academic departments that had secured their standing by making history a science.[67] It was perhaps only natural that

Goode sought them out, given his interest in the history of science and the genealogical investigations that he carried out privately for patriotic societies.[68]

A congressional charter formalized the museum's relationship with the American Historical Association in 1889. Under the terms of its charter, the AHA reported to Congress through the Smithsonian, which published the AHA's annual report. Goode designated Clark as the historians' editor and curator and identified a room in the museum in which to receive their gifts of manuscripts and artifacts.[69] In a related action, Clark used a list of state and local historical societies received from the AHA's Herbert Baxter Adams to solicit historical relics by gift or exchange.[70] Few donations came from either effort.

As officers in the Sons of the American Revolution, both Goode and Clark sought contact with members thought likely to have choice relics. Clark in particular believed that hiring museum employees who were SAR members would multiply the chances of contact, and for a time it seemed that membership in a military or patriotic society was a condition of employment in the Section of Historical Relics. Clark's aide Paul Beckwith, for example, boasted memberships in the SAR, the Society of Colonial Wars, and the First Regiment Minute Men.[71]

Goode had long attempted to unite competing Sons organizations in Washington and New York. Of the two, the New York organization operating as the Sons of the Revolution (SR) applied more stringent qualifications to its prospective members, and its leaders regarded Goode's genealogical methods in Washington as lax. In an unsuccessful effort to knit the SR and SAR into a single national organization, Goode became an officer in both in 1890. A newspaper account of Goode's plan was more successful in catalyzing the female descendants of Revolutionary patriots to unify. Mary S. Lockhart, the proprietor of a Washington, DC, boarding house, took exception to the SAR's consignment of women to the margins of the Revolutionary past.[72] Within a matter of weeks the Daughters of the American Revolution (DAR) formed in Washington. Claiming the mantle of the true spirit of the Revolution, the DAR proposed to unite "battlefield and home" as inspirational historical settings of revolutionary action.[73]

Goode and Clark quickly joined their wives by acting as advisors to the DAR. The National Museum's arrangement with the AHA set the precedent for a congressional charter for the DAR, specifying publication of an annual report by the Smithsonian. Instead of a room, Goode freed up an exhibit case for historical relics in the North Hall of the museum. The DAR's relic deposits were not donations but long-term loans awaiting the construction of a DAR museum—a distant if not uncertain prospect that was not realized until 1913. Among the first depositors was Goode himself, who contributed his great-grandmother's Revolutionary-era spinning wheel. Goode introduced the spinning wheel into a design for the DAR insignia that he patented and signed over to the organization in 1891.[74]

Goode's loan agreement did not prevent the museum from soliciting comparable material for its own collection. But it did prevent donations from the DAR—the group that proved to be the most productive source of Revolutionary relics—from entering the museum's collection, while the hope of receiving relics from the SAR and the AHA remained just that. Goode might have given them display cases as well, had they anything to contribute. The museum received from the SAR only a banquet favor in the shape of a miniature Franklin stove (see page 82) and a brick that an SAR member had collected at Wakefield, George Washington's boyhood home (see page 68 ). The AHA demonstrated no enthusiasm for the reliquarian past whatsoever. The lack of a scientific method with which to study collections rendered futile the museum's courtship of the historical profession; the training of American scholars at that time was influenced by the methods of the German historian Leopold von Ranke, whose empirical approach favored the analysis of manuscripts, not artifacts.[75] However, the manuscripts that were contributed by the AHA proved to be of no consequence and were later sent on to the Library of Congress.[76]

Rejecting artifacts as primary source material, historians remained suspicious of reliquism. The AHA's J. Franklin Jameson, for example, criticized the indiscriminate pile-up of "poke bonnets and spinning-wheels" in state and local historical societies. Jameson might well have been talking about the antiquarian impulse underlying the museum's DAR deposits in general and Goode's spinning wheel in particular.[77]

In his annual report for the Section of Historical Relics in 1894, curator A. Howard Clark reflected upon the need for greater prudence and caution when weighing the significance of the historical relics offered to the museum. Going forward, he explained, the museum would accept only "fully authenticated relics about which definite historical statements may be made." Clark would accept relics, but only if they were the right relics. By 1896 Clark concluded that it would be "advisable to collect as many as possible of such relics, though mere 'curios' are not desirable."[78]

That year George Brown Goode died at the age of forty-five from pneumonia.[79] He never lived to see the DAR exhibit case in the North Hall that displayed his great-grandmother's spinning wheel. At the time of his death, the case had been cleared and was awaiting installation adjacent to George Washington's uniform and a display of colonial-era household effects from New England [Fig. 11].[80]

While Goode cared deeply about the historical past, the taxonomy that he developed was of little use in interpreting it. After Goode's death, Clark and Beckwith carried on his agreements with the DAR, cataloging, displaying, and storing the organization's relics while they awaited a museum of their own. Beckwith's eyesight failed in 1906, and he died the following year. Clark passed away on New Year's Eve in 1918. He maintained his membership in the SAR until the end.[81] In the coming years, it was left to others to bring to a conclusion the policy of "deposit with display," which had permitted organizations to place their artifacts under the museum's care without permanently donating them. Even though the DAR's museum was completed and most of its collections moved into it in 1913, the Smithsonian's storage of its deposits continued until 1931.[82] A similar deposit-with-display agreement that Clark negotiated with the Colonial Dames of America in 1899 lasted until 1924. The last loan was returned in 1932.[83]

In the intervening years, the construction of a new museum building for the Smithsonian's natural history and ethnographic collections relieved the competitive pressures for storage and display space. This new National Museum building, erected

**FIG. 11**

Relics deposited by the
Daughters of the American
Revolution were displayed
in this exhibit case made available
to the organization by the
Smithsonian's George Browne
Goode shortly before his death
in 1896. The case featured
the Revolutionary-era spinning
wheel that had once belonged
to Goode's great-grandmother.

across the Mall from the Castle, opened to the public in 1910. (It is now known as the National Museum of Natural History.)[84]

In 1919 a major Smithsonian reorganization created an independent Division of History that removed the nation's historical relics from under the Department of Anthropology. The split appears to have been an amicable one; it was understood that the emotional value of the museum's relic collection was not consonant with the rational detachment emphasized by the Smithsonian's scientists in their efforts to attract investment, resources, and new buildings.

The job of curating the new division fell to Theodore Thomas Belote, who joined the museum in 1908 and whose interests included armaments, flags, and numismatics. Born on the Eastern Shore of Virginia in 1882, Belote graduated from the University of Richmond and held a master's degree in history from Harvard. Like many historians of his generation, Belote studied at the Universities of Berlin and Leipzig. While an assistant curator, Belote published a definitive catalog of the division's George Washington relics and a popular article in the *Daughters of the American Revolution Magazine* about the division's military collection, which had greatly expanded with the First World War.[85]

Belote grappled with the history-as-science question that weighed so heavily on the study of relic collections. In 1924 Belote shared the dais with historian J. Franklin Jameson at the annual meeting of the American Association of Museums (AAM), held in Washington at the Smithsonian Castle. A champion of the historical museum, Belote stated that the time had passed when its collections could be considered as "merely a sort of junk shop for the care of miscellaneous relics."[86] Revising his talk for publication, Belote described the organization of his division's collection—a system that might be applied to the problems of any historical museum wishing to distance itself from "unscientific" and "heterogeneous" collections that had accrued from "chance donation." Belote's plan emphasized biographical material from well-known figures, followed by antiquarian and household objects; numismatic artifacts; and documentary pictorial material, especially historic scenes, portraits, and photographs. Noting that the historical museum was a relative "newcomer" to the museum field, Belote suggested that even objects found in established art and science museums could contribute "an historical atmosphere" when used to illustrate the progress of civilization. Here Belote drew a firm distinction between the vital association object and the trivial.[87]

In appraising the new historical museum, Belote, of course, had an aging collection with which to work. In addition to the National Museum's presidential relics, which now included Thomas Jefferson's desk, Abraham Lincoln's coat and hat, and Ulysses. S. Grant's state and diplomatic gifts, Belote received the suffragist collections of Carrie Chapman Catt and Susan B. Anthony. He also had the Star-Spangled Banner—the enormous flag flown at Baltimore's Fort McHenry during the War of 1812. Belote installed the flag in a massive case against a long wall in the North Hall.[88] As Belote expanded the notion of a respectable historical museum collection to include relics, they began to be known as *historical objects* and *historical artifacts*.[89]

Near the end of his career, Belote turned to numismatics. The study of coins and medals combined a traditional understanding of history with an appreciation of aesthetics similar to that accorded to fine art. The history collections were lopped off into sizable subdivisions—Military, Naval, and Civil. Belote's portion of a 1941 "index exhibit" (an exhibit mounted in the Castle that was designed to represent the Smithsonian's historical collections) highlighted these new organizational categories on the eve of American entry into the Second World War. The display took on a decidedly martial tone in emphasizing the lives of statesmen and soldiers. The collection illustrated "the interrelationship between the civil, naval and military phases of American history [to] indicate clearly the roles played by many eminent Americans in one or more of these fields of national service."[90] Doubts as to significance no longer burdened the relic as an object class [Fig. 12].

After the war, the Division of Civil History was further divided into Political, Costume, and Domestic divisions. The selective separation of collections from the legacy collection—now known as General History—left a miscellany of relics dating to the

**FIG. 12**

Stylishly designed to dramatize
the museum's administrative plan,
this portion of the 1941 history
index exhibit displayed in the
Smithsonian Castle highlighted
military, civil, and naval collections.
The civil case featured a copy
of Jean-Antoine Houdon's bust
of George Washington and the
portable lap desk on which Thomas
Jefferson wrote the Declaration
of Independence (see page 42).

days of John Varden and the US Patent Office; these were retained by the Division of Political History. In the same period, addressing the declining condition of the museum's storage facilities and exhibitions took on a new urgency. The masking of display conditions in the Arts and Industries Building included coats of paint in "case cream," a color chosen to hide dust. Belote, dispirited by the chronic lack of resources, brushed "historic dust" from certain of the relics in his care, putting it into small envelopes that he labeled and left with the collection. The envelopes read: "dust from G. Washington relics," "dust from Jefferson relics," and so on. As late as 1982, Belote's sarcastically labeled dust packets were misinterpreted as earnestly preserved reliquarian curiosities rather than as a biting comment on the dilapidated condition of the scientific-historical museum whose cause he had championed.[91]

In 1962 a condemnation committee lead by head curator Wilcomb E. Washburn attempted to cull the miscellany left behind by the multiple reorganizations over the years. However, committee members could not bring themselves to jettison even the smallest relics of the museum's recent past, debating the significance of such artifacts as the sugar-cube-size piece of the Bastille. They consigned it to Washburn's office.[92] A graduate of Dartmouth College, Washburn had received his PhD in the history of American civilization from Harvard University in 1955. He joined the museum's staff in 1958, serving as curator of the Division of Political History from 1959 to 1965. He went on to lead the Smithsonian's first Department of American Studies, a position that he enjoyed until retirement in 1996. In his inimitable fashion, Washburn took his fellow intellectuals to task for overlooking the knowledge found in museum objects that he described as *manufacts*, whose significance he believed surpassed manuscripts.[93] Shortly after the new Museum of History and Technology (now the National Museum of American History) opened in 1964, Washburn opened a presidential-campaign exhibit in its Hall of Historic Americans. The new exhibit included a broadcast microphone once used by President Franklin D. Roosevelt to deliver Fireside Chats, collected from a Washington, DC, radio station, which had kept it since the New Deal (see page 142).

In the latter half of the twentieth century, relic collections, which had always been strong in biographical association, were additionally valued as sources of information and comment on museum practices of the past. A 1980 exhibition revisited the history of the National Museum through some of its relic accessions; the tone of the display oscillated between the sarcasm of Belote's dust packets and the earnestness of Washburn's manufacts. Among objects drawn from all parts of the museum, the Division of Political History's contributions included Napoleon's napkin; Varden's presidential-hair collection; a cane made from a floor joist of Independence Hall (see page 50); a stone from Joan of Arc's prison (see page 102); and a letter opener made from the handle of a shovel used in building the Grand Coulee Dam (see page 84). The exhibition's title—*The Nation's Attic*—was received in some quarters as a threat to the Smithsonian's reputation as a scientific enterprise.[94]

Today's Division of Political History collects objects related to the White House, women's history, reform movements, and presidential campaigns. The General History collection—that agglomeration of unclaimed and untaken relics—includes a Plymouth Rock fragment (see page 48), a burned beam from London's infamous Newgate Prison (see page 100), and cake pieces from President Franklin D. Roosevelt's 1934 birthday ball (see page 144).

The challenge remains to identify artifacts with which definite historical statements may be made. Deciding what to collect is a matter of curatorial taste and discretion, within the practical considerations of available space. The museum continues to collect relics, though it calls them something else—*historical artifacts* or *association pieces*. In a world of mediated and ephemeral political occurrences, the museum responds as it is uniquely qualified to do, alighting on things—and pieces of things—that sum up an event or era. Most recently this visual shorthand has included a concrete fragment of the graffiti-covered Berlin Wall (see page 106) and the magnifying glass famously used by Florida judge Robert A. Rosenberg in refereeing the 2000 presidential election ballot recount (see page 154).

★ ★ ★

**T**here is considerable irony among the unclaimed relics of an earlier day, as their value lies in the fact that someone did once claim them. Throughout the life of the museum, new accessions of contemporary objects have joined relics from the darkest corners of the collection to offer object lessons about the ideas that Americans hold about themselves and their country's place in the world. The reproducible mementos that we think of today as souvenirs only partially satisfy a deeply emotional urge to save and connect with a longingly ached-for past. If the past could be touched, it could be chipped away, excavated, carted off, and whittled into pocket-sized bits—giving form to persons, places, and events that lingered forever in the act of possession.

More than a few of these objects can be traced to the collections and cabinets of the individuals who built the National Museum. More surprising is the continuity with the past that can be read in the smallest and most personal of things, in which the real triumph is the survival of the thing itself.

# THE CAUSE
# OF FREEDOM

# Plymouth Rock fragment

## PLYMOUTH, MASSACHUSETTS

—

Gift of the heirs of Mrs. Virginia L. W. Fox, 1911

Plymouth Rock is often described as a figural gateway, an entry point marking passage from the old world to the new. As a relic, this fragment of Plymouth Rock has everything going for it: a painted provenance attributing the piece to a lineal descendant of Governor William Bradford of Plymouth Colony, and even the date and time when it was chipped from the "Mother Rock."

As a geological specimen, Plymouth Rock was once a boulder-size glacial erratic (a non-native rock transported by a glacier) standing out on the otherwise smooth and sandy shoreline of what is now Plymouth, Massachusetts.

According to oral tradition, the Mayflower Pilgrims landed on or near the rock in 1620. Contemporary accounts of the landing, however, make no mention of a rock. In 1741, upon learning of a plan to cover the rock with a wharf on Plymouth's bustling commercial waterfront, Thomas Faunce, a town historian, minister, and acquaintance of the first Pilgrims, recalled hearing the story as a boy. Identifying the rock as the Pilgrim's landing spot, Faunce asked that it not be removed from sight. Thereafter, Plymouth Rock became the focus of Founder's Day orations commemorating the landing of the Pilgrims.

In 1774 well-meaning antiquarians attempted to relocate the rock from the shore to the protection of the Plymouth town square. A team of twenty oxen harnessed for the removal accidentally cleft the rock in two along a horizontal quartz vein. The topmost portion of the rock continued on to the town square while the bottom portion remained behind on the shore. The fragment pictured here was "Broken from the Mother Rock," the name given to the shoreline rock to distinguish it from its breakaway in-town offspring. In 1880 the Pilgrim Society of Plymouth reunited offspring and Mother rocks, cementing them together in a monumental enclosure that had been made for the Mother Rock in 1867. In 1920 the Pilgrim Society moved the entire assemblage a short distance to a new protective cage underneath a waterfront promenade, where it may be seen today.[1]

While no noticeable pieces have been taken from the rock since 1880, earlier pieces and fragments may be found in museums and private collections. None, however, bears such an inscription. This fragment belonged to Gustavus Vasa Fox, a New England antiquarian, diplomat, and assistant secretary of the US Navy. In 1866 President Andrew Johnson dispatched Fox to Russia to convey the president's congratulations to Tsar Alexander II, who had escaped an assassination plot. Fox's Plymouth Rock came to the museum along with his extensive collection of Russian state and diplomatic gifts. It is not known how or from whom he received it.

# Oak cane made from an original floor joist of Independence Hall

## PHILADELPHIA, PENNSYLVANIA

———

Gift of Stockton W. Jones, 1927

The building first known as the Pennsylvania State House is most closely associated with the signing of the Declaration of Independence in 1776 and the Constitutional Convention that ratified the US Constitution in 1787. After 1800 the building's various uses included housing for visiting Native American delegations, a courthouse, the Library Company of Philadelphia, and the Philadelphia Museum of Charles Willson Peale. The designation of the building as Independence Hall did not come into common parlance until the nation's centennial in 1876, although some had used the name since an 1824 reception held for the Marquis de Lafayette in the largest and most prominent room of the building, where the Declaration and the Constitution had been enacted. Originally constructed for the provincial assembly of Pennsylvania between 1732 and 1735, the building was enlarged and altered many times. The most notable addition was the erection of a tower with a belfry in 1753, and in time the building's leading relic became the Liberty Bell (later enshrined in a nearby location of its own).

In 1873 work commenced to turn the hall into a National Museum for Revolutionary Relics.[2] The installation of a new tile floor for the museum involved the removal of fifty-eight original wooden floor joists that were to be cut up and turned into relics. This cane was made from one of those floor joists by the Philadelphia firm of Thomas Wallace and George William Keller, a manufacturer of wooden bar rings. Wallace and Keller purchased Independence Hall wood under an exclusive agreement with the city of Philadelphia. An accompanying affidavit pictures "Independence Hall" and is certified by the mayor of Philadelphia, the hall's supervising contractor, and other luminaries who vouched for the wood's "genuineness."

# Wooden nutmeg and unfinished wood from the Connecticut Charter Oak

## HARTFORD, CONNECTICUT

—

*Nutmeg: gift of W. H. Whitlaw, 1892*
*Unfinished wood: gift of William B. Wetmore, 1913*

The legend of the Connecticut Charter Oak began in 1687, when colonists hid their provincial charter in the hollow of an oak tree to protect the document and their rights from a new regional governor who threatened to usurp them. Like the tree, the legend grew in significance in the era of the American Revolution through the time of the revision of the Connecticut State Constitution in 1818. From time to time a branch of the Charter Oak would fall and would be fashioned into souvenirs. The tree became so celebrated that any small piece of it was prized, whether a limb, a twig, or an acorn—or even a print or photograph. The exclusive access enjoyed by those who possessed pieces of the Charter Oak was literally blown away the night of August 21, 1856, when the mighty tree toppled during a summer storm. The oak's owner, I. W. Stuart, received many requests for pieces of it and attempted to fill every one. In 1856 alone, the distribution amounted to some ten thousand pieces. Though many remained in a raw, unfinished state, many more were turned into conspicuous bric-a-brac. The Hartford, Connecticut, arms magnate Samuel Colt turned the manufacture of Charter Oak relics into a minor industry. Furniture and cabinetmakers also developed lively sidelines producing canes, picture frames, and wooden nutmegs (the Connecticut state symbol).

The firm of Robbins & Winship made this nutmeg from leftover pieces of wood from the governor's chair now exhibited in the State Capitol at Hartford. The prodigious output of the late Charter Oak impressed Hartford's Mark Twain, who noted that there was now enough of it in circulation "to build a plank road from here to Salt Lake City."[3]

# Souvenir Statue of Liberty

## NEW YORK, NEW YORK

———

Gift of Richard Butler, 1885

This is one of the first models of *Liberty Enlightening the World* cast in the United States. Often described as the American Committee Model, this statuette was produced in the tens of thousands. It was sold to subscribers to finance the construction of a pedestal for the original, full-size statue on an island in New York harbor.

Based upon the design of the French sculptor Frédéric-Auguste Bartholdi, with Bartholdi's full cooperation, the miniature statues were produced in six- and twelve-inch sizes. A national newspaper campaign led by Joseph Pulitzer's *New York World* advertised statuettes at one dollar for the six-inch model seen here or five dollars for a twelve-inch version. Richard Butler, a New York–based rubber manufacturer, was secretary of the American Committee of the Statue of Liberty and oversaw the models' production. Butler worked closely with Bartholdi as his American agent in raising the funds for the construction of the pedestal—and in all other matters related to Bartholdi's statue. For both sizes of the model, the subscriber could complete the figure of *Liberty* by placing her on the pedestal, figuratively completing her construction.

Butler's campaign was wildly successful in disseminating likenesses of *Liberty* throughout the United States and the world. The campaign turned the figure into a household souvenir while raising more than enough money for the construction of the monumental stone pedestal through which visitors ascend to the statue's crown and torch.[4] The finished monument was dedicated on October 28, 1886.

THE CAUSE OF FREEDOM

55

# "Jailed for Freedom" suffrage pin

## WASHINGTON, DC

—

Gift of Amelia Himes Walker, 1960

In the summer of 1917, the Nineteenth Amendment circulated through the states. If approved, it would amend the US Constitution to prohibit the denial of the right to vote based on sex, effectively conferring upon women the right to vote. The National Woman's Party (NWP), the most outspoken proponent of the amendment, sought the support of President Woodrow Wilson. When Wilson refused, the party lambasted the president in the pages of its magazine, the *Suffragist*. The party compared the president's lack of action at home with his lofty rhetoric in the defense of democratic ideals and America's responsibilities in the ongoing World War. The party picketed the White House, an unprecedented political act in its time. Carrying banners and signs, some eighty-nine women activists were arrested by the District of Columbia police and incarcerated in the city's workhouse at Occoquan, Virginia.

While serving time at Occoquan, Alice Paul, the founder and leader of the NWP, sketched the design for the pin that became a symbol of the party's struggle. The pin replicated in miniature a jail-cell door, with a tiny chain clasped with a heart-shaped locket. The "Jailed for Freedom" pin resembled the so-called "Holloway" suffrage brooch attributed to the activist Sylvia Pankhurst, which Paul had seen in England. It was finished to Paul's specifications by Nina Allender, an artist whose work regularly appeared in the *Suffragist*. Convening at a Washington, DC, theater the following year, the party distributed the pins to honor what it hoped would be its "last picket line" of members who had been arrested outside the White House.

This particular pin was awarded to Amelia Himes Walker, a suffragette who recalled first meeting Alice Paul at Swarthmore College. Walker gave her pin to the museum in 1960, along with a reminiscence of being one of the women who picketed and were arrested at the White House on Bastille Day (July 14) in 1917. Walker had carried a banner inscribed "Liberty, Equality, and Fraternity." After five minutes, she and fifteen other picketing suffragettes were arrested and taken to police court, where they were charged with "obstructing traffic," a ruse to detain the picketers. Refusing bail, the suffragettes were on trial for two days. They were sentenced to sixty days in jail but were released after a few days at Occoquan.[5] Congress ratified the Nineteenth Amendment on August 18, 1920.

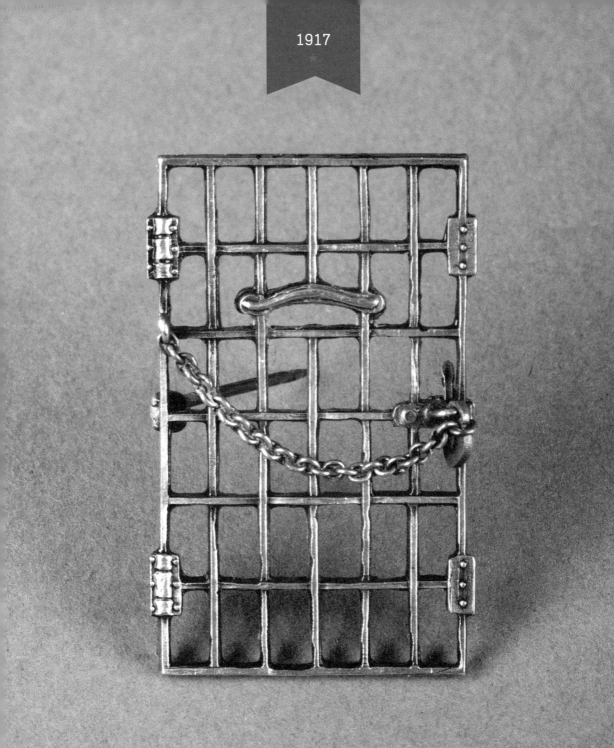

# THE
# IMMORTAL
# WASHINGTON

# Piece of George Washington's mahogany coffin

## MOUNT VERNON, VIRGINIA

---

Purchase, 2011

An act of vandalism at the family burial vault of George Washington in 1830 set in motion a plan to construct a new and more secure tomb at Mount Vernon. The old vault had been set into a hillside overlooking the Potomac River, not far from the mansion. Architect William Strickland, with Washington's nephew Major Lawrence Lewis and others, moved Washington's remains to a new tomb not far from the old vault in 1837. When Strickland and Lewis entered the old vault to remove Washington's coffin, its wood broke away in pieces, leaving the remains sealed inside what had been the coffin's lead lining. Strickland noted that in the thirty years since Washington's death in 1799, the wooden part of the coffin had been renewed three times. James Green, an Alexandria, Virginia, cabinet-maker, was hired to make what is believed to have been Washington's third and final coffin, which Strickland and Lewis placed in a marble sarcophagus in the new tomb in 1837.

Their plan had been to make souvenirs from the mahogany coffin wood, but its deteriorated condition made that idea unworkable. Small pieces of the wood, however, were distributed. The note on this piece reads "Washington's Coffin presented to Mr. Saltonstall by a nephew, + namesake of Washington residing at Mount Vernon."

The Saltonstall to whom the note refers is believed to be Leverett Saltonstall, representative from Massachusetts to the US House of Representatives from 1838 to 1843. Saltonstall often visited Mount Vernon; as early as 1825, he hoped that Mount Vernon's buildings might be kept in better repair, but "never be modernized or lose the features given them by W." Saltonstall found Washington's burial vault "an object of indescribable interest… in the most romantic spot imaginable—very near the river—at the edge of the bank—upon which Washington no doubt loved to roam." Saltonstall noted that two limbs of the cedar trees growing over the vault had been "sacrilegiously sawed off" by visitors, the others "mutilated." Without irony, he enclosed two cedar sprigs with his letter, promising to bring more home soon.

Saltonstall visited Mount Vernon again in 1840, when he likely received this coffin piece from John Augustine Washington, George Washington's great-grandnephew and Mount Vernon's resident owner. Saltonstall was also acquainted with Washington's grand-nephew Colonel George Corbin Washington of Georgetown. Whether Saltonstall obtained his souvenir from Augustine, Corbin, or another Washington nephew is open to conjecture. Saltonstall did not elaborate on the circum-stances of his 1840 visit to Mount Vernon.[1]

# Wooden George Washington plaque from James Crutchett's Mount Vernon Factory

## WASHINGTON, DC

Purchase, 2010

Inspired by patriotic interest in the construction of the Washington Monument, Englishman James Crutchett produced souvenir George Washington keepsakes in his "Mount Vernon Factory." Previously known for illuminating the US Capitol with gaslight, Crutchett contracted in 1852 with John Augustine Washington, the last of the president's family to live at Mount Vernon, to harvest wood from his estate for the purpose of making souvenirs. The contract specified wood from the vicinity of Washington's tomb and an outlying tract. Crutchett's Mount Vernon souvenirs came with a certificate of authenticity issued under the authority of Crutchett; John Augustine Washington; and the mayor of Washington, DC.

Crutchett modeled an initial run of souvenir canes after the president's favorite walking stick. He later made many more saucer-shaped, wooden-framed engravings picturing Washington and his tomb and mansion. Crutchett dedicated half of the proceeds from sales to the Washington National Monument Society, the other to himself. As a business venture, however, Crutchett's souvenir sales floundered by the early 1860s, as construction stalled on the monument that had inspired his undertaking. Beset by creditors, Crutchett's idled factory and its wooden inventory were seized by the federal government at the beginning of the Civil War to be made into a soldiers' rest near the capital's railroad passenger station. Making a public appeal for relief to President Lincoln in 1861, Crutchett recommended his souvenirs as rewards of merit for the nation's children. His appeal to Lincoln was unsuccessful. Returning to the gas industry after the war, Crutchett later sought to revive his souvenir business in the 1880s with Washington wooden-medallion sets, but was never able to regain his footing. He was unable to capitalize even upon the opening of the Washington Monument in 1888. He died penniless in Washington, DC, in 1889.[2]

# Old ivy from Mount Vernon

## MOUNT VERNON, VIRGINIA

—

Gift of Mrs. Frederic W. Huidekoper, 1909

Souvenir sales were developed at Mount Vernon as an alternative to the depredations of tourists determined to take pieces of it. Estate-made souvenirs capitalized upon natural features including vines, flowers, and trees, which were renewable and could be cut to bits and even written upon at the mansion's greenhouse.

This piece of ivy belonged to Mr. and Mrs. Frederic W. Huidekoper of Washington, DC. Frederic W. Huidekoper was a prominent figure in the American railroad and steel industries and in the city's Burleith neighborhood west of Georgetown. A booster of Washington, DC, Huidekoper relocated the headquarters of the railroads that he consolidated near the city's monumental core. Huidekoper is believed to have shared his wife's interests in genealogical research as members of the Society of Colonial Wars and the Daughters of the American Revolution. Their piece of Mount Vernon ivy came to the museum along with his collection of geological specimens, gathered throughout the country during his railroad and steel days. Though the museum's scientists pronounced the ivy "worthless," nevertheless, it was graciously accepted as part of the collection at the wishes of the donor.

# Washington Monument cornerstone piece

## WASHINGTON, DC

—

Transfer, Library of Congress, 1961

Broken from the cornerstone of the Washington Monument laid in 1848, this piece of marble with the monument's painted image belonged to Joseph Meredith Toner, a Washington, DC, physician, philanthropist, and amateur historian. Heavily involved in the intellectual life of the nation's capital, Toner collected all things related to George Washington, helped found the Columbia Historical Society (now the Historical Society of Washington, D.C.), and led the revival of the commission in 1884 that oversaw the completion of the monument in 1888.

Gifts of stone played a crucial part in the monument's construction, including the 24,500-pound marble cornerstone, laid at the northeast angle of the foundation before an audience of 15,000 to 20,000 people on July 4, 1848. Begun by private subscription, the construction came to a halt for lack of funds in the mid-1850s. Not until the nation's centennial in 1876 did Congress resume work on what in the intervening years had become a national embarrassment.

The restart began with a feasibility study of the monument's foundation that led to its expansion to support a freestanding masonry obelisk with a height of 555 feet. The new foundation covered the cornerstone, whose below-grade location can now only be approximated.

Master mechanic P. H. McLaughlin, known as "Monument" McLaughlin, oversaw the work on the grounds. Representing the monument committee, Toner was present the day that McLaughlin and his crew shored up the cornerstone, and it was McLaughlin who presented Toner with a piece of it that broke off in the process. Dr. Toner took great pride in showing it. "I am not a vandal," he later volunteered to a reporter, who noted that Toner bundled his prize in a gauzy bandage "wrapped around the small chunk of marble as carefully as the swaddling clothes around the ghostly form of an Egyptian mummy."[3] It is not known who painted the stone.

THE IMMORTAL WASHINGTON

# *Brick collected at Wakefield,*
# *George Washington's boyhood home*

COLONIAL BEACH, VIRGINIA

—

Gift of John Paul Earnest, 1898

This clay brick came from the site of George Washington's earliest home on the banks of Popes Creek, near the present-day city of Colonial Beach, Virginia. Born in 1732, Washington lived there until the age of three, when his parents, John Augustine and Mary Ball Washington, moved to Mount Vernon. The farm, which they left to family members, became known as Wakefield in the 1770s. The property suffered a disastrous fire in 1779 and was abandoned. Over the years, the elements and pillaging relic hunters reduced the ruins of the house and its outbuildings to obscurity. One of the home's two standing chimneys fell apart and was salvaged for new construction. A second was picked apart by parties of picnickers "that landed on the sandy beach confiscat[ing] the bricks and stones for souvenirs until but few remained."

President Andrew Jackson dedicated a small obelisk at the farm site in 1833. Not until the 1890s did renewed interest in Washington's birthplace as a patriotic shrine compel the organization of a memorial association to oversee its preservation. President Grover Cleveland visited to dedicate a new obelisk in May 1894. The cornerstone of the older and smaller obelisk

that Jackson dedicated in 1833 was worked into the base of the new shaft. "Relic brokers" gathered the leftover bits from the original obelisk to sell to visitors "at twenty-five and fifty cents apiece, according to size."

Ongoing efforts to identify the foundation of Washington's actual birth-house led to further excavation of a debris pile that recommended itself to visitors seeking pieces of the Colonial past. John Heltz, a member of the Sons of the American Revolution who visited the site in September 1894, collected this brick from debris that may or may not have been part of the house's foundation. Heltz acquired his relic before the War Department finished excavating one of the two chimney foundations in an attempt to discover the dwelling's footprint. Subsequent archaeological investigation in 1941 revealed that a memorial hall built in the 1920s on what was thought to be the original foundation had missed the mark. Presenting the appearance of a home, it nonetheless became a modern Colonial-revival shrine.[4]

The brick is the gift of John Paul Earnest, a George Washington University law professor who donated it to the museum in his capacity as the secretary of the National Society of the Sons of the American Revolution.

# Miniature compass embedded in a nut from Mount Vernon

## MOUNT VERNON, VIRGINIA

—

Gift of Laura Wolcott Tuckerman (Mrs. Willard G. Treist),
Ruth Hollingsworth Tuckerman, Margaret Cary Tuckerman,
Elsie Tuckerman, and Alice Noel Tuckerman, 1961

This nut is believed to have fallen from one of Mount Vernon's buckeye trees. George Washington is known to have collected buckeye seeds at the mouth of the Cheat River in the present state of West Virginia in 1784 and planted them on his estate the following year. A census of the trees in the vicinity of the mansion published by the Harvard botanist and arborist Charles Sprague Sargent in 1917 identified seven buckeyes located along the serpentine paths of the estate's bowling green—a finely-kept lawn edged with trees that Washington devised to shade and frame the approach to the mansion.

The buckeye has been embedded with a miniature compass and fixed with a ring so that it may be worn as a charm. It is a transitional piece in the late-nineteenth-century economy of commercial souvenir production, which was changing from locally to globally produced material—in this case, a nut from Mount Vernon was combined with a compass from nowhere in particular. The playful juxtaposition of the buckeye from Washington's estate and the compass suggests its potential for providing historical and moral direction.[5]

This compass nut came to the museum with curiosities donated by the Tuckerman sisters and their families of Washington, DC. Their donation included a membership badge from the Association for the Preservation of Virginia Antiquities; a badge celebrating the Jamestown, Virginia, Tercentenary of 1907; and an engineer's tripod and level used to survey the boundary of Alaska and Canada in the 1910s. Their donation also included a photograph from a series of Mount Vernon views picturing visitors at the turn of the twentieth century.

# Wooden compotes made from the Washington Elm

## CAMBRIDGE, MASSACHUSETTS

—

Gift of Mrs. Leonard Carmichael, 1976

These small, wooden compotes, or cups, were turned from a piece of the legendary Washington Elm, under whose branches George Washington was said to have accepted his commission as the head of the Continental Army in Cambridge, Massachusetts, on July 3, 1775. For many years the legend was believed to be true and grew along with the storied tree at the intersection of Garden and Mason Streets near Harvard Square. On October 26, 1923, the tree, long dead but carefully attended by the city's arborists, toppled into the street. The Cambridge police quickly cordoned off the tree to protect it from relic hunters who arrived armed with saws; arborists cut up the trunk and branches and carted them away to a local warehouse for safekeeping until the city decided what to do with the wood. In response to requests received from all corners of the country, the city sent a labeled slab cut from the trunk to each state governor, with two gavels made from branches going to each state legislature. A specially polished piece of the trunk was sent to Mount Vernon. The city distributed the remaining slabs and unfinished pieces to the public, exhausting the supply. Many pieces were left to the turn of woodworkers and hobbyists, who created their own memorials. In 1927, for example, the city presented aviator Charles Lindbergh with a miniature of his aircraft, the *Spirit of St. Louis*, modeled from the supply.

Though the Washington Elm legend was subsequently denounced as apocryphal by the Cambridge Historical Society, efforts to set the record straight ran into a Parson Weems–like wall of misattribution that lingered into the 1930s. The legend continued to live on, even after the arboretum at Harvard University joined in the debunking effort when nurserymen began selling grafts said to have been propagated from the Washington Elm and urged public planting as a lesson in patriotism by civic and school groups.[6]

These small compotes are believed to have been turned by a private woodworker from the supply of Washington Elm wood given away by the city. They were given to the museum by the wife of Smithsonian Secretary Leonard Carmichael, who, before coming to the institution, was the president of Tufts University in Medford, Massachusetts.

# INDUSTRIAL REVOLUTIONS

# Medal box made from wood carried on the Seneca Chief at the opening of the Erie Canal

NEW YORK, NEW YORK

—

Gift of Henry Adams, circa 1890

The preservation of the historical past was once the domain of painting, sculpture, and the medallic arts. By the 1820s souvenir mementos and keepsakes had begun to take on the functions of more traditional art in monumental civic celebrations such as the opening of the Erie Canal in 1825.

The completion of the canal linked the Great Lakes to the Atlantic Ocean in a continuous water route via the Hudson River. Souvenir tickets, badges, medals, and wooden medal boxes made to be distributed among local, state, and national officials (including current and former presidents of the United States) symbolically linked the east and west and the past and present. The *Seneca Chief*, the first boat to travel the length of the canal to New York City, was thoughtfully stocked with "curious woods" from "western forests."

Pieces of cedar as well as birdseye and curled maple were put in an "aboriginal canoe" from Lake Superior and ceremoniously placed aboard the *Seneca Chief*. Arriving in New York, the wood was finished into souvenir medal boxes by leading artisans: wood turner Daniel Karr and cabinetmaker Duncan Phyfe. The inside top of each box carries the crest of the city, with the legend "Presented by the City of New York." The inside bottom carries the legend "This box was made of a piece of wood, brought from Erie in the first Canal Boat the Seneca Chief."[1]

This particular box, made from curled maple, is believed to be the gift of Professor Henry Adams of Harvard University, the historian and great-grandson and grandson, respectively, of medal recipients John Adams and John Quincy Adams.

THIS BOX
was made of a piece of
wood, brought from Erie
in the first Canal Boat
THE SENECA CHIEF.

# Wooden chip cut from a railroad tie

## PROMONTORY, UTAH

—

Gift of Hart F. Farwell, 1922

Traveling west with his mother in June 1869, eight-year-old Hart F. Farwell stopped at Promontory, Utah, to cut a chip from a special railroad tie. The previous month, on May 10, 1869, the ceremonial "Golden Spike" had been driven into a "last tie" to complete the first transcontinental rail link in the United States.

The joining of east and west by rail was a significant event in American life and culture. Aside from the relative economy of freight and the pleasures of rail passenger travel (which the Farwells enjoyed), the realization of a national network of iron, steel, and steam, as represented by the Golden Spike, became a unifying metaphor in the years after the Civil War. The ceremony featured four spikes as well as the special tie. The first, the Golden Spike, was engraved for the Pacific Railroad; a second, lower-grade gold spike was supplied by a San Francisco newspaper; the state of Nevada supplied a silver spike; and the Arizona Territory supplied a blended iron, silver, and gold spike.

Farwell's donation of his chip to the National Museum caused Smithsonian Secretary Charles D. Walcott to wonder what had become of the first Golden Spike. Walcott's friend Robert S. Lovett, the chairman of the board of the Union Pacific Railroad, confirmed the story of the ceremony and the spikes, but could not authenticate the tie that young Farwell had sampled some weeks later. The tie originally driven with the spikes had been specially milled and predrilled for the occasion from California laurel wood. That laurel tie had been removed immediately after the ceremony and replaced with a pine tie no different from the rest. Lovett noted that even as the laurel tie was being removed, it "suffered seriously at the hands of relic seekers." Some years later the laurel was discovered in the shop of the Southern Pacific Company in Sacramento, California. The railroad removed it for safekeeping to its San Francisco headquarters, where it was unceremoniously destroyed with the entire building in the earthquake of 1906.

A travel writer confirmed that the souvenir whittling began at the ceremony and never let up. After the removal of the ceremonial laurel-wood tie, "a charge was made on the last tie by relic hunters, and soon it was cut and hacked to pieces, and the fragments carried away as trophies or mementoes of the great event.... Weeks after the event we passed the place again, and found an enthusiastic person cutting a piece out of the last tie laid. He was proud of his treasure—that little chip of pine, for it was a piece of the last tie. We did not tell him that three or four ties had been placed there since the first was cut in pieces."[2] The wooden chip that Farwell cut from the tie in the weeks after the ceremony was his lifetime possession.

# Piece of Mississippi bedrock from beneath the east pier of the St. Louis Bridge

## ST. LOUIS, MISSOURI

—

Gift of the heirs of Mrs. Virginia L. W. Fox, 1911

This small piece of stone is a memorial of one of the great engineering achievements of the nineteenth century—the construction of a bridge spanning the Mississippi River at St. Louis. The St. Louis Bridge, alternately know as the Eads Bridge in tribute to its chief engineer, James B. Eads, provided a vital link between Illinois and the east and St. Louis and the west. The bridge's design pioneered the use of cantilevered steel; its steel spans arced out across the river from two stone piers built midstream, sunk bedrock-deep below the sand and soil of the riverbed.

The nature of the river's sandy bottom had long been a matter of debate and conjecture. Eads's decision to sink the piers to bedrock drew from firsthand experience, for he had walked the bottom of the turbulent river, observing its ever-shifting swirl of sand and sand-scoured bedrock. Eads had grown up with little formal education and had become a clerk on a Mississippi River steamboat. He became keenly interested in salvaging the cargoes of sunken riverboats that, once abandoned, could be claimed for the taking. He devised a diving bell with an air hose in which he walked and felt his way along the bottom of the river, raising cargo by hand. In time he was able to salvage entire boats using specially constructed barges, cranes, and sand pumps,

and became very rich. During the Civil War, Eads became acquainted with Assistant Secretary of the Navy Gustavus Vasa Fox, after suggesting mechanical improvements to the turret guns of the Union Navy's ironclad river-boats. The shallow-draft boats soon cleared the Mississippi of Confederates from Vicksburg to New Orleans. Fox later invested in Eads's St. Louis Bridge and related railroad ventures, whose success Eads assured Fox was "ironclad."

Taking no chances, Eads sunk his bridge piers to bedrock at a time when others speculated that sand would be sufficient. From barges with cranes, masons laid stone on the framework of a caisson, pushing it into the sandy riverbed. Eventually this required the attention of workers in an air lock at the bottom of the caisson, accessed by a spiral staircase from the top. The work was dangerous and the effects of a swift ascent resulted in "the bends," whose cause was not at the time known.

The caisson of the east pier on the Illinois side of the river reached bedrock, "127 ½ ft. below high water mark and 80 ft. under sand," in January 1871.[3] Eads sent Fox a drawing of the bridge at his request and appears to have followed up by sending Fox this piece of bedrock cut from the riverbed inside the caisson.

Mississippi bed rock from beneath east pier St. Louis Bridge, 127½ ft. below high water mark and 80 ft. under sand.

# Miniature copper model of the Franklin Stove

## NEW YORK, NEW YORK

—

Gift of the Sons of the Revolution through Henry Russell Drowne, 1907

This miniature copper model of the cast-iron fireplace or stove devised in 1741 by Benjamin Franklin was given in 1906 as a souvenir of the annual banquet of the New York chapter of the Sons of the Revolution. Though attributed to Franklin, the stove's design was improved upon by Philadelphia inventor David Rittenhouse, who added a slanted fireback to improve heat radiation and an L-shaped flue that drew off smoke more effectively.

Made to be a match holder, the metal party favor bears the Sons' embossed insignia with the inscription "Feb 22, 1906—Franklin Stove 1742." The Sons of the Revolution banquet attracted some six hundred members and an impressive list of invited guests representing national patriotic and historical societies to the spacious, flag-draped hall of Delmonico's Restaurant on the night of George Washington's birthday. The guests included members of the Friendly Sons of St. Patrick; the Saint Nicholas Society; the Society of the War of 1812; the New-York Historical Society; the Society of Colonial Wars; the Holland Society; St. George's Society; St. Andrew's Society; and the Colonial Order of the Acorn. Though the banquet's ostensible purpose was to mark the birthday of the immortal Washington, one after-dinner orator noted, "The year belonged to Franklin."[4] It was the bicentennial of Benjamin Franklin's birth, marked with a toast to his memory and a stove at each place setting.

# Letter opener made from a shovel used in building the Grand Coulee Dam

## SPOKANE, WASHINGTON

—

Transfer, Library of Congress, 1977

The construction of the massive Grand Coulee Dam west of Spokane, Washington, beginning in 1933, came to symbolize the vigorous planning and vital action of the New Deal. Historically described as the quintessential "shovel-ready project," the damming of the Columbia River for irrigation, flood control, and hydroelectric power had been discussed for decades.

So large was the project that it was carried out in stages. Work commenced on a low dam that eventually extended to a height of 553 feet, just 2 feet short of the Washington Monument's height. The following construction of the high dam was sent out for bids in 1937 and was completed in 1941, on the eve of America's entry into the Second World War.

This letter opener, made from a used shovel handle, belonged to Harold L. Ickes. As secretary of the interior under President Franklin D. Roosevelt, Ickes oversaw the dam's construction by the US Bureau of Reclamation. Roosevelt visited the construction site with Ickes on August 4, 1934. Ickes publicly aligned himself with the construction of Grand Coulee and addressed a nationwide radio audience from Washington, DC, on the opening of construction bids for the high dam in 1937.

FDR again visited the site that year in an open touring car. Ickes, a champion of the New Deal's public electric-power-generation projects and a frequent lecturer on reclamation issues, would have had plenty of opportunities to come into possession of this souvenir during his subsequent dam visits in 1938 and 1941.

As in many of its other engineering projects throughout the West, including the Boulder (later Hoover) Dam, the Bureau of Reclamation constructed parking lots and turnouts for visiting tourists. At Grand Coulee, these adjoined a private concessionaire who sold souvenirs of the largest concrete structure in the world—the so-called "Biggest Thing on Earth"—which had transformed the Columbia River basin into a giant agricultural-industrial project.[5] The construction was memorialized with the smallest of souvenirs, such as Ickes's letter opener. The Bureau of Reclamation often produced such items, and individuals (construction contractors, for example) also produced them for limited distribution. Secretary Ickes left the Department of the Interior in 1946; his letter opener was transferred to the museum in 1977 from his manuscript collection at the Library of Congress.

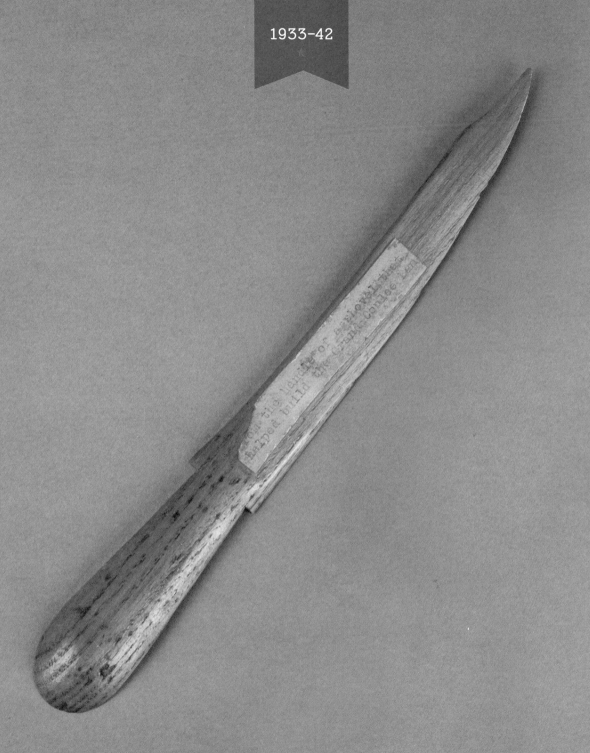

# FOREIGN GUESTS

# Piece of the Bastille

## PARIS, FRANCE

—

Gift of Mrs. Sarah Ella Cummings, 1924

Cataloging this small metal cube in 1924, curator Theodore T. Belote described it as a "piece of the Bastille at the time of its overflow."

The storming of the Bastille, a former royal garrison and prison in the city of Paris, on July 14, 1789, was a seminal event in the history of the French Republic and a Revolutionary symbol that has been celebrated in Franco-American relations ever since.

The demolition of the Bastille left a debris field as long and wide as the burgeoning market for Revolutionary relics in France, England, and the United States. The Marquis de Lafayette, for example, presented George Washington with a key to the Bastille that Washington proudly displayed in the center hall at Mount Vernon. Another key was prized by the historical novelist and collector John Galsworthy.[1] In 1964 the Smithsonian's Condemnation Committee considered disposing of its Bastille relic, but no one could think of an "appropriate agency that would accept this tiny cube."[2] Unlike the structure from which it came, the tiny cube escaped condemnation as a loan to the head curator's office.

# Napoleon's napkin

The Emperor Napoleon gave this table napkin to William Bayard on February 26, 1815, the morning Napoleon left exile on the island of Elba, off the coast of Tuscany, Italy. The napkin is embroidered in one corner with a small green crown above the letter *N* and in the opposite corner with the red initials *W.B.* William Bayard, a wealthy American who traveled widely on the continent among the courts of Europe, had called upon the exiled French emperor, who reportedly invited Bayard to join his party returning to France. Instead, Bayard came home with his story and two of the emperor's napkins.

William Bayard and his family enjoyed a large circle of acquaintances who loomed large in national life and culture. Bayard's father witnessed Alexander Hamilton's death in the aftermath of his ill-fated duel with Aaron Burr in 1804. The senior Bayard chaired the New York committee to receive the Marquis de Lafayette in 1824 and the following year chaired the meeting that arranged the New York City celebration of the opening of the Erie Canal.[3] Throughout Bayard's life, relics played a significant role as social currency, perhaps none more so than this linen napkin.

Bayard gave both napkins to Lucy Hunter Churchill, the wife of US Army Inspector General Sylvester Churchill. Mrs. Churchill, the future mother-in-law of Smithsonian Secretary Spencer Fullerton Baird, was a keen admirer of Napoleon's executive ability. The napkin pictured here was bequeathed to the museum by the Bairds' daughter, Lucy Hunter Baird, in 1914.

# Lady's glove with a portrait of the Marquis de Lafayette

## UNITED STATES

—

Gift of Mrs. E. M. Chapman, 1912

The Marquis de Lafayette traveled the United States on a farewell tour from 1824 to 1825. The outpouring of public affection for the Revolutionary hero and friend of George Washington left a trail of commemorative silk ribbons, transfer-print ceramics, household wares, and gloves emblazoned with Lafayette's likeness.

The popularity of commemorative gloves was a source of consternation for the "Nation's Guest," who was shocked to see his own portrait on the ladies' hands that he was obliged to accept with a kiss. When offered a gloved hand at a ball in Philadelphia, Lafayette "murmur[ed] a few graceful words to the effect that he did not care to kiss himself, he [then] made a very low bow, and the lady passed on."[4] The glove pictured here has lost its provenance; it was perhaps separated from its mate as a keepsake.

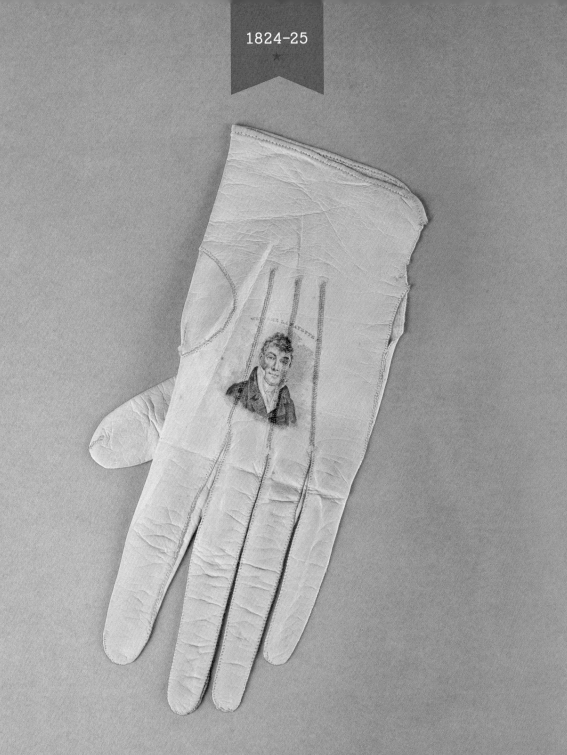

# Lock of Sir Walter Scott's hair in a glass vial

## MELROSE, SCOTLAND

———

Gift of George Ainslie, 1882

This lock of hair was cut from the gray head of the Scottish poet and historical novelist Sir Walter Scott. The lock was cut by Scott's daughter Anne during his last illness at Abbotsford, his home in the Scottish highlands. Scott's physician gave the lock to Hew Ainslie, Scott's former Abbotsford neighbor and a celebrated Scottish poet in his own right.

Ainslie had emigrated to the United States in 1822, eventually settling in Louisville, Kentucky, where he opened a branch of a successful Midwestern brewery in 1829. Ainslie is best remembered for *Scottish Songs, Ballads, and Poems* (1855), in which he recounted his struggles in his native land and the opportunities afforded him in his adopted land. Ainslie never wrote in any other than his native Scottish dialect, which made it difficult for most Americans to read his work. In Scotland, however, he achieved the status of a celebrity. On his literary tours of Scotland, Ainslie was welcomed as a national hero, the quintessential Scotsman made good.

Ainslie had returned to Scotland and was there on the occasion of Sir Walter Scott's death in 1832. Ainslie attended Scott's funeral. His preservation of a lock of Scott's hair was in keeping with the antiquarianism that Scott himself had polished to perfection during his life at Abbotsford—with its romantic interiors made to look old and outfitted with arms, trophies, and leather-bound books, all of which reflected Scott's success as the leading dramatist and interpreter of the Scottish historical past.[5] After Hew Ainslie's death in 1878, his son George, US congressional delegate from the territory of Idaho, donated Sir Walter Scott's lock of hair to the National Museum in a carefully sealed and labeled glass vial.

# Railroad conductors' punch cards

## WORLDWIDE

—

Bequest of Homer N. Lockwood, 1913

These four stock cards bearing railroad conductors' punch marks were collected by Homer N. Lockwood. The inscription written by Lockwood on one card explains: "These four cards, punched, I carried with me throughout the United States, thence to Mexico afterwards around the world, and thus preserved punch marks of the Railroad Conductors of the Globe." One card is autographed by President Benjamin Harrison, its reverse by President Porfirio Diaz of Mexico. Another carries the autograph of Sanford B. Dole, a Hawaiian Islands lawyer and jurist.

Lockwood served one term in the New York State Assembly and later became the director of two small regional railroads in upstate New York. Between 1852 and 1865, however, Lockwood made the most of his circumstances by adding to his collection of punch marks as a traveling salesman for the cartographer J. H. Colton, a publisher of guidebooks and maps of the United States and the West Indies. During Lockwood's tenure with the company, Colton published the *Traveler and Tourist's Route-Book through the United States of America and the Canadas* (1854). A wealthy man who left the bulk of his considerable estate to charity, Lockwood bequeathed to the museum a collection including rare coins, wooden canes, a marble model of the Taj Mahal, and a mahogany curio cabinet filled with unmounted gems, carvings, enamels, lacquers, pottery, bronzes, inlaid work, embroidery, and scarabs.[6] Lockwood's punch marks came in a well-traveled leather slip case of the kind carried in a suit-coat pocket.

# Piece of mosaic pavement from the palace of Tiberius

## ROME, ITALY

—

Gift of George Hans Boehmer, 1886

This tiny piece of travertine marble was taken from the mosaic pavement of the palace of the Roman emperor Tiberius by George Hans Boehmer, director of the Smithsonian's International Exchange Bureau. Trained as an anthropologist, Boehmer began his scientific career with the National Weather Service (at that time a division of the US Army Signal Service) in the early 1870s and later joined the Smithsonian, where he used his translation skills to track developments in astronomical observatories around the world.

In the early 1880s Boehmer worked as a special agent to expedite exchange agreements for scientific publications with foreign governments. Aside from the usual difficulties and delays that complicated overseas shipping, the timely exchange of publications was sometimes met with indifference by these governments, and so, Boehmer traveled to Europe in 1884 as a representative of the Smithsonian and the Library of Congress.[7]

While in Italy, Boehmer visited the ruins of the palace of Tiberius, built for the Roman emperor on Palatine Hill in the first century AD. Boehmer explained that he collected this piece of mosaic pavement in 1884 but had kept it for a while before giving it to the museum. The little piece of pavement that Boehmer pocketed on Palatine Hill perhaps meant more to him than the pallets of books that he had expedited to Washington. Though Boehmer's souvenir had little value as an antiquity, the museum's Division of Ethnology nevertheless accessioned it as a gift.

**1884**

3582
Accession *17.178*
SMITHSONIAN INSTITUTION,
WASHINGTON, D. C.
OFFICIAL BUSINESS.

Any person using this card to avoid the payment of postage on private matter will be subject to a fine of $300.

REGISTRAR'S FIL
Return to Registra...

A piece of Mosaic pavement from Tiberius Palace, Palatine Hill, Rome, Italy, taken up, Decbr. 3. 1884 by and presented, Febr. 13. 1886 to U.S. National Museum by

Jr. J. Bossum

# Section of oak beam from the Newgate Prison chapel

## LONDON, ENGLAND

—

Gift of P. C. William Fulcher, 1905

The demolition of London's notorious Newgate Prison might have passed into memory without notice had it not been for the work of Charles Dickens. As architecturally impressive as it was bleak, Newgate's high-walled squalor spawned a Dickensian literary genre of its own, the so-called Newgate novel. Newgate appeared in Dickens's earliest reporting on London's social conditions, collected in *Sketches by "Boz"* (1836), and as a setting in his novels—notably, *Oliver Twist* (1838) and *Barnaby Rudge: A Tale of the Riots of 'Eighty* (1841). Dickens's enduring popularity on both sides of the Atlantic led readers to seek out the places drawn in his sketches and novels. After his death in 1870, a flood of transatlantic tourists made their way to "disappearing Dickensland," as one traveler described the vanishing London sites.

Newgate Prison, hard by the site of the London Wall built by the Romans, had been the place of a city jail since 1188. Newgate exercised a curious pull upon the young author. In *Sketches by "Boz,"* Dickens described the prison's low doors, interior yard, and arrangements for visits with prisoners who ranged from debtors to felons to murderers. The murderers came to an end through execution by hanging. Dickens paid particular attention to the arrangements of the Newgate Prison chapel—the "bare and scanty pulpit," the gallery for women inmates with its "great heavy curtain," the men's with "unpainted benches and dingy front," "the tottering little table at the altar," and the "great black pen" of a pew in which the condemned sat next to his own empty coffin for the Sunday service preceding his execution.

Dickens's descriptions contributed to Newgate's dispersal far and wide when the prison closed for demolition in 1903.[8] London Police Constable William Fulcher obtained this piece of an oak beam from the chapel, which had burned during the 1780 "no Popery" Gordon Riots that Dickens had dramatized in *Barnaby Rudge*. Fulcher carried it with him to the British pavilion at the Louisiana Purchase Exposition (the St. Louis World's Fair) in 1905, from which he wrote to the secretary of the Smithsonian Institution with the offer of its gift.

# Stone from the dungeon of Joan of Arc

## ROUEN, FRANCE

—

Gift of the Joan of Arc Statue Committee through George F. Kunz, 1915

On the eve of the First World War, an equestrian statue of Joan of Arc was raised in New York City. The cast-bronze figure was placed atop a pedestal fitted with stones recently excavated from the castle in which she had been imprisoned and led to the stake in 1431. The statue and its symbolic pedestal were the inspiration of the American Scenic and Historic Preservation Society (ASHPS), led by George Frederick Kunz. Born in New York in 1856 and raised in Hoboken, New Jersey, Kunz was educated at New York's Cooper Union, where he studied mineralogy. As a gemologist with Tiffany and Company, Kunz rubbed shoulders with J. P. Morgan and Thomas Edison, who shared Kunz's interest in saving the city's historic buildings, as well as his desire to dot the city with new historical monuments.

A campaign for the beatification of Joan of Arc came to public attention in 1909, when Kunz chartered a statue committee to commemorate the upcoming five hundredth anniversary of the birth of the Maid of Orléans in Domrémy, France, in 1412. Kunz organized an exhibition about Joan of Arc. The exhibition, which ran from January to February of 1913, raised two-thirds of the necessary money for the statue and served the double purpose of gathering visual and historical material (from collectors including Morgan and department store magnate Rodman Wanamaker) on which to model it. Kunz's statue committee chose the young sculptor Anna Vaughn Hyatt to create the figure of an armor-clad Joan astride a horse, standing upright in the stirrups, her right arm raised high with a sword. Kunz explained that Hyatt's work would be "the first equestrian statue of the Maid by a maid."

The so-called dungeon stones incorporated in the statue's pedestal aroused great curiosity, and Kunz, never one to allow a symbol to lie fallow, explained their origin. In 1912 he had learned of the availability of these stones, which were being excavated to make way for the foundation of a modern building in Rouen, France. With the help of the French historian Jean de Beaurepaire, Kunz and the statue committee purchased the lot of 229 blocks, some 36,000 pounds of stone. Kunz vouched for the stones' authenticity as "thoroughly certified." The stones left Rouen for New York in June 1914, a little more than a month before the German invasion of Serbia and the outbreak of the First World War. Today they form the decorative elements of the pedestal of the statue at Riverside Drive and Ninety-Third Street, visible in their original unfinished condition on its east end and fashioned into Gothic panels inset on its north and south sides.[9]

**DUNGEON STONE**

FRAGMENT of one of the 229 blocks of fossiliferous limestone weighing 18 tons from the Dungeon of Joan of Arc in Rouen, France, forming part of the pedestal of the statue of Joan of Arc dedicated December 6, 1915, on Riverside Drive at 93d Street, New York City. The Dungeon was demolished in March, 1914, to make room for a modern building.

# Souvenirs from the cabinet of
# Abby Knight McLane

## WASHINGTON, DC

—

Bequest of Abby Knight McLane, 1919

The objects pictured here are souvenirs collected by Abby Knight McLane and her husband, Allen McLane. The well-traveled couple is thought to have personally gathered the collection, which represents the kind of curio-cabinet collecting that occupied many Americans in the last decades of the nineteenth century.

The McLanes had ample opportunities to travel throughout the United States and abroad. A graduate of the US Naval Academy, Allen McLane joined the Pacific Mail Steamship Company after his service and eventually became the president of the line until about 1870, when he retired to make a tour of Europe with his wife. The couple returned to live in Baltimore and New York, until settling in Washington, DC, in 1880. Allen McLane died in 1891.[10] Abby Knight McLane bequeathed the collection to the museum at

the behest of her friends Rose Gouverneur Hoes and Cassie Mason Myers Julian-James, two Washington society women then assembling a collection of first ladies' gowns for the museum.

Though each piece of McLane's cabinet is unique, as a souvenir collection it is a typical mix of found and historical association objects: "antediluvian oak" from a bog near Killarney, Ireland; a stone from the ruins of Pompeii, Italy; a metal fragment of the HMS *Great Britain*, the vessel used in the laying of the Atlantic Cable; a piece of a cedar doorpost from Government House in St. Augustine, Florida; and a stone in the shape of an arrowhead from the top of Mount Pony, near Culpeper, Virginia. The collection was assigned to the Division of Ethnology and exhibited in the Smithsonian Castle in a case arranged by Mrs. Hoes.

Piece of cedar door-post of the Government-House, St. Augustine, Fa: built in 1562: The wood from Cuba.

From the top of Pony Mountain near Culpeper, Virginia

Antediluvian Oak from a bog near Killarney.

# Concrete fragment of the Berlin Wall

## BERLIN, GERMANY

—

Purchase, 2011

The opening of the twelve-foot-high Berlin Wall by the East German government on November 9, 1989, signaled the collapse of Communism and led to the reunification of East and West Germany. Their separation through the center of Berlin dated to the Allied partition of the country into occupied zones after the Second World War. The literal and figurative walling off of Eastern Europe from the West was first described as an "iron curtain" by Winston Churchill in 1946. By 1948 the Soviet Union sealed the East German border, creating a crisis for the sustenance of 2.5 million West Berliners. Within a matter of days, the successful American airlift of supplies into West Berlin circumvented the blockade. By 1961 the flight of refugees caused the East German government to create an expanse of no-man's land between high walls and fences. President John F. Kennedy appeared near the wall in June 1963, delivering a speech in which he attacked the Soviet Union with his famous declaration, "I am a Berliner." In June 1987 President Ronald Reagan demanded that Soviet Premier Mikhail Gorbachev "tear down this wall."[11]

When the end came, portions of the wall were cut into memorial-size chunks. An apparently limitless supply of smaller bits recommended themselves to a global audience who had witnessed the wall's destruction on television. This concrete fragment, for example, was sold by a German flea-market vendor in Berlin to a visiting Canadian student, who in turn sold it on an Internet auction site.

# DIPLOMACY
# AND WAR

# Vase made from a timber of the USS Constitution

## BOSTON, MASSACHUSETTS

—

Gift of Edna T. Sheldon, 1994

The functional equivalent of a seagoing Mount Vernon, the USS *Constitution* left in its wake transmogrified timbers, masts, decks, and hull planks after an 1833 renovation. Beloved as "Old Ironsides" (for the strength of its wooden hull), under the command of Isaac Hull during the War of 1812, the *Constitution* destroyed the British frigate *Guerriere*, the first time an American ship had defeated a British ship on the high seas. The sinking of the *Guerriere* was as much a turning point in the history of the war as in the historical development of the US Navy.

In 1833 Hull returned to the command of the *Constitution* to oversee its stem to stern renovation at Boston's Charlestown Navy Yard. Hull ordered that the wood removed from the frigate be set aside to produce souvenirs and memorials for a grateful nation. Enough wood was removed from the ship to make a phaeton carriage for President Andrew Jackson; a baptismal font for a Boston church; and canes, picture frames, snuffboxes, cups, and vases to be bestowed upon naval officers and public officials.[1] A silver plaque set in the base of this wooden vase is inscribed:

> This Vase, made from an original timber of the U.S. Frigate Constitution built in 1797, was presented to Sarah F. Gray by Lieut. Babbit [*sic*], U.S. Navy, 1835.

Lieutenant Edward Babson Babbitt was stationed at the Charlestown Navy Yard near the end of his seagoing days, where he was engaged in the renovation of ships. Babbitt gave the vase to Sarah Frances Loring, who married William Gray in Boston in 1834; with its elaborate inscription, the vase may have been a wedding gift. The vase descended through their family and was given to the museum in 1994.

# Mexican-American War spoils

## AMOZOC DE MOTA, MEXICO
—

Gift of Mrs. Harrison Howell Dodge, 1906

This collection of war souvenirs was found by Lieutenant William Henry Browne in what he described as a "ruined house" believed to be near the present-day Mexican city of Amozoc de Mota in the state of Puebla. Just eighteen years old at the beginning of the Mexican-American War, Browne was assigned to the US Army command of Major Winfield Scott. Scott's forces bombarded the city of Veracruz before marching inland to occupy Mexico City. Browne saw action along the way at Cerro Gordo, Contreras, Molino del Ray, and Chapultepec. Scott's forces engaged the Mexican army in house-to-house combat, breaking through walls to access occupied rooftops, where parapets offered cover for small-arms fire.

Following the war, Browne mustered out of the army to practice law and drew upon his experiences in Mexico in developing a reputation as a poet and raconteur. In 1853 he published "The Mexican Coquette," a short story about an American army officer bivouacked in a monastery and later a church that has been turned into a hospital after the battle of Mexico City. Reflecting upon the country's conquest by the Spanish conquistador Fernando Cortés, Browne's protagonist is forced to reconsider his own role as "an enemy and an invader."

Browne later served with distinction in the Civil War, raising fourteen volunteer companies from New York and attaining the rank of general. Returning to his law practice after the war, Browne became an authority on trademarks, publishing a highly regarded text on the subject in 1873.[2] Browne died in Washington, DC, in 1900, leaving his modest collection to his wife, Louise Wolcott Knowlton Browne, who placed it on loan to the museum in 1901. The museum exhibited the checkerboard paper, embroidered rose on paper, carved wooden cross, and rosary in a case in the rotunda of the Arts and Industries Building. After Mrs. Browne's death, her sister, Mrs. Harrison Howell Dodge of Mount Vernon, donated the collection, including Browne's swords and related war materiel, to the museum.

# Towel used as a flag of truce

## APPOMATTOX COURT HOUSE, VIRGINIA

—

Bequest of Elizabeth B. Custer, 1936

This towel is half of the flag of truce that was carried between Confederate and Union battle lines to effectively end the American Civil War at Appomattox Court House, Virginia, on April 9, 1865. Made from a white towel with red stripes, the flag was improvised and carried by Confederate horseman Captain Robert Moorman Sims. Waving the towel-flag above his head as he approached the Union lines, Sims sought to deliver a note from Confederate General Robert E. Lee to Union General Philip H. Sheridan asking Sheridan to halt his advance upon the Confederates until Lee could meet with General Ulysses S. Grant. Sims first encountered Union General George A. Custer, who stated that nothing but unconditional surrender would be considered by Grant. Custer allowed Sims to carry this message back through Union lines to the Confederate position, in the safe company of Union Lieutenant Colonel Edward Washburn Whitaker and another Union officer now unknown.

Sims recalled that on their way back to the Confederate position, Whitaker asked him "if I would give him the towel to preserve that I had used as a flag." Sims refused. He told Whitaker that he would see him "in Hell first," not wishing to see the flag preserved "as a monument of our defeat." Whitaker apologized, saying that he had not intended to offend. A different Confederate officer who was to return Whitaker safely to the Union line requested to borrow the flag. Sims took him aside and explained that under the circumstances, he would lend the flag, but that it was not to fall into the hands of the Federals—that is, the relic-minded Whitaker.

This, of course, is exactly what happened. The accompanying officer later told Sims that "Colonel Whitaker asked for the towel to display to keep his own people from firing on him, and, as soon as he got into the lines, he mixed up with the others and disappeared with the towel." Later that day, Lee surrendered to Grant at Appomattox Court House. Whitaker cut the flag in half, giving one piece to Mrs. George A. Custer with an affidavit that he wrote at Appomattox the day after the surrender. Whitaker kept the other half for himself. A small portion cut from it is said to have been placed in Grant's tomb.[3]

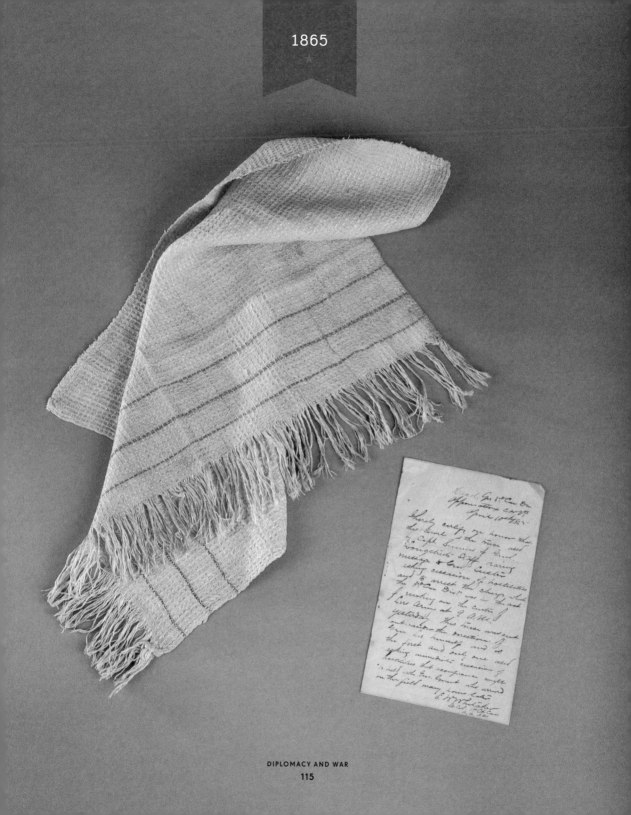

# Table and chairs used by Robert E. Lee and Ulysses S. Grant

## APPOMATTOX COURT HOUSE, VIRGINIA

—

Bequest of Wilmon W. Blackmar, 1906; gift of Bridget O'Farrell, 1915;
bequest of Elizabeth B. Custer, 1936

The Civil War propelled the practice of relic hunting to new heights. While leading artists of the day revisited battles in cyclorama paintings and monumental sculptures, battle-hardened soldiers documented the history unfolding before their very eyes with everyday objects. This caned maple armchair, pine-top side table, and leather-covered office chair were taken from the home of Wilmer McLean in Appomattox Court House, Virginia. There, on April 9, 1865, General Robert E. Lee surrendered to General Ulysses S. Grant, effectively ending the war.

With Grant's Union Army victorious, the chairs and table used by Grant and Lee to execute the surrender terms were quickly seized and taken from McLean's home by Grant's officers. For an unknown sum (if any) Colonel Edward Washburn Whitaker took the caned maple armchair that Lee used. For twenty dollars in gold, General Philip H. Sheridan left with the table that Grant and the two commanders' military secretaries used to prepare the surrender document. Sheridan, who purchased the table as a present for George A. Custer's wife, Elizabeth, waited outside the McLean house for Custer, who soon came upon the scene, swung the table over his shoulder, and galloped away with his wife's prize. For ten dollars in gold, General Henry Capehart left with the leather-covered office chair that Grant used; Capehart's aide, Captain Wilmon W. Blackmar, placed Grant's chair across his saddle and rode off.

The Appomattox furniture acquired the status of national relics. Near the end of his life, Henry Capehart gave the Grant chair to Blackmar, an avid collector of Civil War memorabilia. Blackmar lent the Grant chair to the Connecticut Historical Society and exhibited it at Grand Army of the Republic (GAR) meetings. E. W. Whitaker gave the Lee chair to a Hartford, Connecticut, GAR encampment, which offered it as a prize to the member selling the most tickets to a theatrical benefit featuring the chair as a stage prop. The contest winner, Captain Patrick O'Farrell, then retired Lee's chair.[5]

Of the three Appomattox furniture owners, Wilmon W. Blackmar was the first to give the Smithsonian the nod, in 1906. Elizabeth B. Custer lent the table to the museum in 1912. Patrick O'Farrell's widow, Bridget, donated the Lee chair to the museum in 1915, reuniting the relics fifty years after the war to reunite the nation.

# Punch bowl, executive mansion of the Confederacy

## RICHMOND, VIRGINIA

—

Transfer, US War Department, 1867

This Limoges punch bowl is one of two taken from the executive mansion of the Confederacy by the US War Department in 1865. It became the property of the United States under Secretary of War Edwin M. Stanton, who, after the fall of Richmond, ordered the confiscation of Rebel government property, including everything from paper records to punch bowls.

Stanton had competition. The Richmond *Whig* reported:

> The fortune hunters turned out…intent upon hunting up and appropriating any little record, scrap of history, relic or memorial that might serve to adorn the pages of history, or fill a niche in the museum of the curiosities of the "Great Rebellion"— its rise, progress, decline and fall, with souvenirs of authors and leaders.

The War Department is believed to have transferred its elegant Confederate punch bowls to the National Museum in 1867, as part of a complex accession spread across multiple museum divisions, including military ordnance and tools, miscellaneous American Indian items, and mineral specimens.

The punch bowls were not formally accessioned until 1984.[4] Prior to its official accession, this one—the most viable of the pair—was brought out of storage, dusted off, and returned to service at the Division of Political History's annual holiday office party.

# "Swords into Plowshares" paperweight designed by William Jennings Bryan

## WASHINGTON, DC

———

Gift of National Trust for Historic Preservation, 1962

This paperweight in the form of a plow was designed by and made for William Jennings Bryan. The unsuccessful three-time Democratic Party candidate for president served as secretary of state under President Woodrow Wilson from 1913 until his break with Wilson in 1915 over Germany's sinking of the Lusitania and the deteriorating relations between the two nations (which led to American entry into the First World War in 1917). During Bryan's two-year tenure as secretary of state, he negotiated thirty treaties with foreign governments providing for a cooling-off period to investigate all disputes. Each of the treaty signatories received from Bryan a copy of this paperweight in the form of a plow, inscribed with a prophecy from the book of Isaiah: "They shall beat their swords into plowshares."

Bryan's paperweights were, in fact, made from steel swords condemned by the US War Department and melted down by the Washington, DC, ordnance factory of the US Navy Department. The factory cast them as plows and plated them with a shiny nickel finish. Bryan stated that the inscriptions were his own contributions "to diplomatic phraseology." Bryan coined "Nothing is final between friends" in the discussion of the anti-alien land laws of California. "Diplomacy is the art of keeping cool" (inscribed on the reverse), was the inspiration for the thirty treaties.

Bryan also distributed his plows to the Washington diplomatic corps, President Wilson, and each cabinet member. As ex–secretary of state, Bryan distributed souvenirs to select state governors and public officials in the hope that they would display the souvenirs in their state capitals. After America's 1917 entry into the war that many had long regarded as inevitable, one Washington diplomat dryly noted, "And the plowshares shall be beaten into swords."[6] Bryan inscribed this plowshare for President Woodrow Wilson on August 13, 1914.

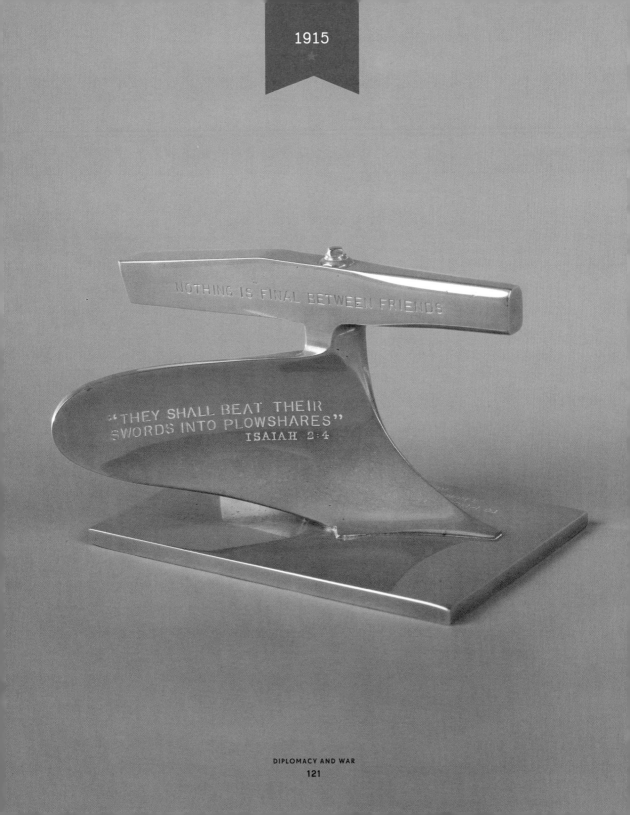

NOTHING IS FINAL BETWEEN FRIENDS

"THEY SHALL BEAT THEIR
SWORDS INTO PLOWSHARES"
ISAIAH 2:4

# Fountain pen used to sign the final armistice agreement for the First World War

## BRUSSELS, BELGIUM

—

Gift of Lewis L. Strauss, Jr., 1979

The cease-fire ending the First World War commenced November 11, 1918, and is traditionally celebrated as Armistice Day. Delegates representing the United States and Great Britain, France, Belgium, and Germany used this pen to sign the final armistice agreement in Brussels, Belgium, on March 14, 1919. Led by the American delegate and future president of the United States, Herbert Hoover, the final armistice settled the terms of the surrender, addressing matters related to German shipping and the Allies' provision of foodstuffs to Germany.

Hoover's secretary, Lewis L. Strauss, provided his personal fountain pen for the signatories' use. Strauss later wrote, "Because of an incurable addiction to the collecting of mementos, my fountain pen was available when the Final Armistice Agreement was ready to be signed and, since the pen was my property, I kept it." Born in Charleston, West Virginia, in 1896, Strauss first worked as a traveling shoe salesman before he volunteered to work for Hoover, who was then the volunteer director of the United States Food Administration under President Woodrow Wilson. Strauss's wartime friendship with Hoover began Strauss's long and successful career in banking, cancer research, and Washington, DC, policy circles, culminating with his appointment as chairman of the Atomic Energy Commission in 1953.[7] In addition to his armistice pen, Strauss's gifts to the museum include a Hoover presidential medal, a pen used by President Dwight D. Eisenhower to sign the Atomic Energy Act, a silver cigarette case from Richard Nixon, and miniature ivory and jade elephant figures. Strauss died at his home in Brandy Station, Virginia, in 1975.

With this pen the final Armistice Agreement was signed by the Allied and German delegates in Brussels Belgium 8:14 ℗.m. March 14 1919

# PRESIDENTIAL
# PIECES

# Wooden chip from the building in which Andrew Jackson studied law

## SALISBURY, NORTH CAROLINA

——

Gift of Mrs. Harrison Howell Dodge, 1906

As a young man, Andrew Jackson studied to become a lawyer with Judge Spruce Macay in Salisbury, North Carolina. This strip of wood was cut from the modest frame-and-shingle office that housed Macay, his law practice, and Jackson from 1784 to 1786. The site of Macay's office is near the present-day Rowan Public Library in Salisbury, North Carolina.

This souvenir is perhaps all that remains of the structure. In 1876 a speculator purchased the building with plans to exhibit it as a memorial to Jackson at the Philadelphia centennial celebration. Dismantled and ostensibly packed onto a railroad car bound for Philadelphia, the wooden building failed to appear at the celebration and has since been given up for lost.[1] The modest size of this small sliver, inserted through the back flap of a business envelope (erroneously marked "'74"), suggests that it may have been sliced from the building long after Jackson's appearance there in 1784, but long before it was dismantled in 1876. That no other pieces are known to have survived suggests that the dismantled wood receded into obscurity, escaping even the notice of relic hunters.

A chip from the building in which
Genl Jackson (Presit) began to practice
law — Salisbury N.C. Apr. 7 '74

# Framed lock of
## Andrew Jackson's hair with note

### NEAR NASHVILLE, TENNESSEE

—

Gift of Ralph E. Becker, 1970

In 1845 Fred Sumner and Colonel William H. Polk, the brother of President-elect James K. Polk, visited former President Andrew Jackson at Jackson's home, the Hermitage, near Nashville, Tennessee. Sumner and Polk were on their way to witness the inauguration of Polk's brother, a friend and political ally of Jackson's, in Washington, DC. Despite Jackson's advanced age, Sumner and Polk found the former president in good spirits. Receiving his guests from a lounge chair, Jackson explained that he was well enough to walk about, but had difficulties breathing and did not expect to live long. Hearing this news, Sumner made a special request:

Could he have a lock of hair for his wife? Right in front of his visitors, Jackson cut a lock of hair from his head and gave it to Sumner.[2] Later that day Sumner wrote up the experience on a piece of blue scrap paper, which he kept with the framed hair lock and its inscription: "—Hermitage—Andrew Jackson's hair given by him to me on 7th Feby 1845." It was a request that Jackson often satisfied at the expense of his personal appearance. On one occasion in 1842, for example, Jackson entertained some two hundred schoolgirls, who according to one reporter, "procured so many of his snow white locks as to give his head the appearance of having just passed from the hands of the barber."

*Hermitage —*
*Andrew Jackson's hair*
*given by him to me*
*on 2d Feby 1845*
*Chrd Sumner*

# Hair of Persons of Distinction and Hair of the Presidents

## WASHINGTON, DC

—

Transfer, United States Patent Office, n.d.

These carefully preserved locks of hair were assembled by John Varden, the keeper of collections who was simultaneously employed by the National Institute for the Promotion of Science and the National Gallery of the US Patent Office. Varden began the collection in 1850.[3] In 1853 Varden made his first display, the *Hair of Persons of Distinction,* from donations that he personally solicited, purchased, or repurposed from existing collections. Though it does not appear to be complete, the *Hair of Persons of Distinction* features the notable locks of Professor Samuel F. B. Morse, sculptor Clark Mills, Generals Winfield Scott and Sam Houston, Senators Henry Clay and Jefferson Davis, and other luminaries.

Varden likely cannibalized his first display to make a second exclusively of presidential hair from George Washington to Franklin Pierce. The reverse panel of its frame is inscribed, "No 1 the Property of John Varden of Washington City September 1855." Varden entered the

*Hair of the Presidents* in competition at the Mechanics' Fair of the Maryland Institute in Baltimore in 1853 and again in 1855.

In 1858 Varden left the employment of the National Institute and the Patent Office to work for Smithsonian Secretary Joseph Henry, whose interest in transferring scientific specimens from the Patent Office to the Smithsonian Museum did not extend to national relics. It cannot now be determined when the two collections left the custody of the Patent Office, or whether Varden continued to consider them his personal property, as he did in lending them to the mechanics' fairs. Nevertheless, the label of Varden's *Hair of Persons of Distinction* suggests the wide range of personal contacts and acquaintances that Varden enjoyed as a museum official. It bears what may be the longest-extant public appeal of its kind preserved in today's Smithsonian: "Those having hair of Distinguished Persons will confere [sic] a Favor by adding to this Collection."

# Fence rail split by
# Abraham Lincoln and John Hanks

## DECATUR, ILLINOIS

—

Bequest of Leverett Saltonstall, 1983

This fence-rail piece is one of the many souvenirs made for the friends and political supporters of presidential candidate Abraham Lincoln. This particular piece is attributed to Lincoln's cousin and rail-splitting partner, John Hanks. It was sold by his cousin Dennis F. Hanks at the Northwest Soldiers' Home Fair at Chicago in May 1865. The second of two Civil War–era Chicago sanitary fairs conceived to raise money for the charitable relief and care of soldiers, this fair, which opened a little more than a month after Lincoln's assassination in April 1865, was especially poignant for its display of the log cabin that Abraham Lincoln and his Hanks cousins had built for Lincoln's father near Decatur, Illinois, from 1829 to 1830. John and Dennis Hanks set up shop in the cabin and sold fence-rail sections and other wooden relics made from them.

The original selling of the martyred president as a frontier rail splitter, however, was the work of Richard J. Oglesby. Later governor of Illinois, Oglesby had organized the Republican state convention that had made Lincoln the party's nominee for president in 1860. Lincoln's nomination was attributed to Oglesby's image management.

Oglesby had arranged for John Hanks and another supporter to carry two fence rails onto the convention floor. The gambit reframed Lincoln the wealthy railroad attorney as Lincoln the rail-mauling day laborer—a ploy that worked in ways that Oglesby did not anticipate. Demand for fence rails soared.

Oglesby found himself on the procurement end of a fence-rail business, identifying and cutting rails and writing affidavits for the illiterate John Hanks, who authorized Oglesby to put his $X$ on a letter that accompanied each rail.[4] By 1865 the job fell to Dennis F. Hanks, who did read and furnished the affidavit for his cousin's $X$.

This fragment of fence rail's subsequent owners contributed their own signatures to cards that they tacked to the wood. The rail's first owner, S. W. Shorey (a Chicago inventor who produced boot-making equipment), purchased it from Dennis Hanks at the Soldiers' Home Fair in 1865. Shorey moved to Allston, Massachusetts, where the rail became the property of Henry Weston, the state guard in the Hall of Flags at the Massachusetts State House. In 1941 Weston's widow gave the rail to Governor Leverett Saltonstall.

This is to Certify that this is one of the Genuine Rails Split By A Lincoln and myself in 1829 and 30 John Hanks ⟨his mark⟩ D F Hanks witness

# Laura Keene's bloodstained cuff, worn at Ford's Theater

## WASHINGTON, DC

—

Gift of Virginia Adler Thompson through George Richard Thompson, 1962

Laura Keene, the actress and theatrical producer, was born in England in 1826. She emigrated to the United States in the early 1850s, where she helped to establish New York City as a leading center of theatrical production.

A theater was eventually constructed for her in New York, Laura Keene's New Theatre (in use from 1856 to 1863); it was there that *Our American Cousin* debuted in 1858. The romantic comedy, centering around an inheritance, caricatured an English lord, his American cousin, and a beautiful dairymaid. After more than one thousand performances of the play and faced with declining audiences for theater in New York during the Civil War, Keene toured her company, alighting in Washington, DC, for a two-week engagement during which she produced and appeared in a changing schedule of plays at the theater of John Ford.

There on the evening of April 14, 1865, the sometime actor and full-time secessionist John Wilkes Booth assassinated President Abraham Lincoln as Lincoln watched *Our American Cousin* from a box above and to the right of the theater's dress circle. Booth was not in the play. But he was familiar enough with the theater to gain access to the President's box and familiar enough with the play to anticipate the audience's laughter

that masked the report of a pistol—fired at point-blank range at the back of Lincoln's head. Making his escape from the box to the stage, Booth brushed past Keene, who had been waiting in the wings to make her entrance.

In the ensuing pandemonium, Keene attempted to quiet the audience from the front of the stage. An urgent call came from the box requesting water for the president. Keene ran off stage for water and then up the theater's south staircase to the second floor, where the president lay. She held Lincoln's head in her lap. Though it was not immediately apparent where the wound was, it soon bloodied her costume, face, and hands and was absorbed in her cuff. She led the way for the men carrying Lincoln out of the theater.

Keene retired for the night to a local hotel. Presuming the worst, she did not learn the outcome until the following day. Visited at the hotel by her husband's nephew, M. J. Adler, she told him what had happened and gave him her bloodstained cuff. A Georgetown hardware merchant, Adler kept her cuff in a business envelope that he later annotated with her story. The cuff passed to Adler's daughter, Virginia Adler Thompson.[5] After her death her son donated it to the museum as a gift in her name.

# Miniature Wedgwood creamer from the White House

## WASHINGTON, DC

—

Gift of Emanuel Newman, 1970

This miniature creamer from a toy Wedgwood tea service once belonged to the children of President and Mrs. Grover Cleveland. Made by England's Wedgwood Company in the early 1890s, the creamer features the stylized Greek, Roman, and Etruscan scenes made popular by the company's line of full-scale ceramic jasperware.[6]

Wedgwood conferred its miniature toy sets upon the children of British royalty, a favor extended to the White House children of the Clevelands. Dr. Emanuel Newman of Falls Church, Virginia, donated the miniature creamer to the museum in 1970. Newman had received it as a gift from the nurse (whose name is now unknown) who had taken care of the Cleveland children until they left the White House. The creamer had been given to her as a memento because its handle had broken; she had kept the creamer and handle in her possession until presenting them to Newman prior to her death in 1946. The museum reattached the handle and added the tiny creamer to its display of White House china in the First Ladies Hall.

# Piece of a stud with a nail
## from the East Room of the White House

### WASHINGTON, DC

—

Transfer from the United States Patent Office, 1902

For three weeks during the summer of 1902, White House visitors combed through architectural debris deposited on the mansion's North Lawn. The renovation of the White House's East Room and conservatories left remnants of various improvements of years past to be eagerly identified, fussed over, and carted off. One reporter identified bits of cornices put in by either First Lady Julia Grant or First Lady Caroline Harrison, as well as the gilded cornice installed by Harriet Lane Johnston, the niece of James Buchanan who served the bachelor president as White House hostess. Relic hunters especially sought ornamental plasterwork, hand-cut wood lathe, and studs and cut nails dating to the mansion's original construction.[7]

Until the grounds were closed at the request of the construction superintendent, neither the pleasures of a Sunday afternoon Marine Band concert nor the pressures of a meeting with President Roosevelt could dissuade tourists, visiting dignitaries, or enterprising relic hunters from sampling the pile.

With the exception of the attached affidavit, the provenance of this stud with a nail from the East Room is now unknown. It is believed to have been cut to size, planed, and labeled by one of several enterprising relic hunters who built a market for collectibles from White House remnants, one stud at a time.

Piece of Studding taken from the East room of the "White House" July 1st 1902. One side of this piece was planed after it was taken out. The nail is one of the old style lath nails (used in 1790) The White House was first occupied in the year 1800.

# Fish-shaped can opener used on Theodore Roosevelt's African expedition

## NAIROBI, BRITISH EAST AFRICA

—

*Smithsonian African Expedition, 1910*

This fish-shaped can opener went to Africa with Theodore Roosevelt. It was deposited in the National Museum with game and natural-history specimens that Roosevelt and his party collected for the Smithsonian, which helped finance and staff the safari. The collection includes anthropological material, mammals, birds, reptiles, fishes, mollusks, marine invertebrates, geological specimens, and material deemed "not of ethnological significance," including Roosevelt's camp chest, an iron hatchet, and this can opener.

A keen enthusiast of "vigorous blood-stirring out of doors sport," Roosevelt began planning his African safari well before he retired from the presidency at the age of fifty in 1909. Roosevelt specified the contents of each provision box, as he had for his hunting trips in the Dakota Territory as a young man. He ordered up cans of Boston baked beans, California peaches, and tomatoes, all "in memory of [his] days in the West."

The African porters engaged for the journey did not consume Roosevelt's nostalgic canned goods, but carried them. The porters ate the same freshly killed meats enjoyed by the rest of the party—after the animals had been skinned and preserved by taxidermists to be transported by rail from Nairobi, then on to the National Museum.

Roosevelt's son Kermit, who accompanied his father, described three "sorts or periods of enjoyment" of their hunting trips. First "is when the plans are being discussed and the outfit assembled…the second is the actual enjoyment of the trip itself; and the third is the pleasure of retrospection when we sit around a blazing wood-fire and talk over the incidents and adventures of the trip."[8]

A rudimentary yet essential tool from the journey that Roosevelt had long imagined, the can opener is of cast iron, inset with a small steel blade. The original finish appears to have been golden paint, worn by heavy use.

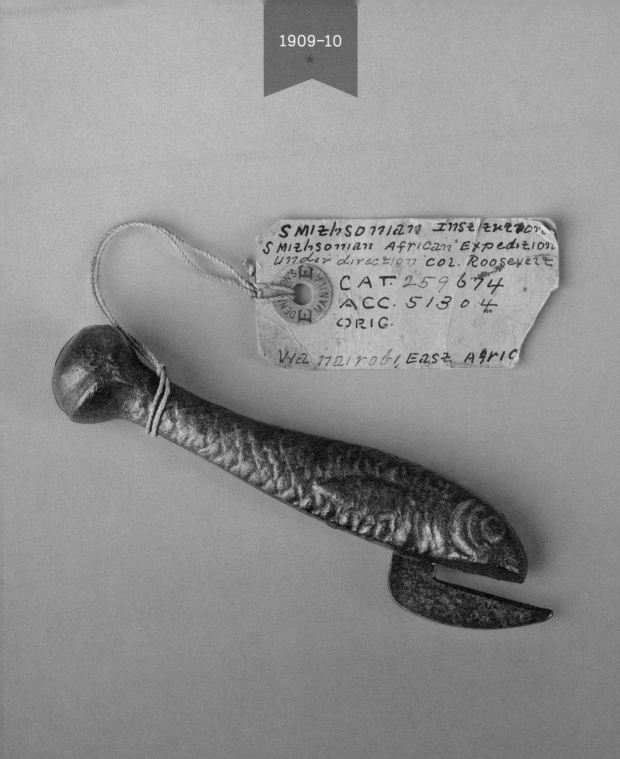

# Franklin D. Roosevelt's Fireside Chat microphones

## WASHINGTON, DC

———

Gift of Columbia Broadcasting System and WTOP Radio, 1960
Purchase, 1996

A master of timing and tone, President Franklin D. Roosevelt built an audience for radio talks, known as "Fireside Chats," in the 1930s. Seated before a forest of microphones, FDR imagined his audience individually. In return, his audience believed him to be personally responsible for their personal wellbeing and improvement.

The name "Fireside Chat" was coined by CBS vice president Harry Butcher at the outset of the New Deal, when Roosevelt first took to the air to explain the changes taking place in the banking system. FDR delivered some thirty Fireside Chats over the course of his presidency from 1933 to 1945. The "CBS" and "NBC" signs bolted to their respective microphones became a familiar feature of newspaper press coverage of FDR's talks. NBC executives insisted on white call letters on a black background, as white letters were more difficult for competing news organizations to remove from photographic negatives.[9]

As broadcast technology improved, the networks retired the microphones to the souvenir shelves of their Washington, DC, staff announcers and engineers. The CBS microphone was found at the network's Washington, DC, affiliate in 1960, where it had been kept by longtime staff engineer Granville Klink. The museum purchased the NBC microphone from an antique dealer, who obtained it from the family of the late Carleton Smith, the network newsman who introduced FDR's talks and is sometimes described as the first White House radio correspondent.

# Cake pieces from
# Franklin D. Roosevelt's birthday ball

## WASHINGTON, DC

—

Gift of Tillie N. Oberheim, 1984

These small, boxed pieces of birthday cake are souvenirs of the president's birthday ball held in Washington, DC, on January 30, 1934. Public-relations specialist Carl Byoir conceived the idea of a ball to raise money for charitable purposes, changing ideas about philanthropic giving in the Great Depression.

The campaign was created to endow the charitable foundation that President Franklin D. Roosevelt created at Warm Springs, Georgia, for the treatment of polio victims. Stricken by polio in 1921 at the age of thirty-nine, Roosevelt purchased the springs and an inn in 1926 after taking the buoyant waters in an effort to rehabilitate his ravaged legs. With the onset of the Depression, however, the foundation that he created to run it fell on hard times. Byoir, who had a modern understanding of how special events could be used in public relations efforts (Byoir had been a publicist with the Committee on Public Information during the First World War), developed a fund-raising campaign tied to a nationwide celebration of the president's birthday.

The campaign featured some six thousand birthday balls held in thirty-six hundred communities throughout the United States on January 30, 1934. Nationally the campaign grossed more than one million dollars. These cake pieces are souvenirs of the birthday ball staged that evening at Washington, DC's Shoreham Hotel. Comedian Will Rogers hosted the celebration, which featured a half-dozen orchestras, headlined by Eddy Duchin and the National Symphony, with dancing and continuous floor shows in multiple ballrooms. The party was attended by twenty-five hundred elegantly attired guests, including members of the military, who came in full-dress uniform. Most guests could not see Eleanor Roosevelt cut the large, multicolored birthday cake, which was obscured by the clutter of lights illuminating the event for the newsreel cameras. Later in the evening, the president joined the festivities in progress across the nation by network radio hookup.[10] These two boxes of cake were taken home from the Shoreham by the parents of Tillie N. Oberheim, who donated them to the museum.

# Photograph, Dewey-Truman necktie poll, Harvey's department store

## NASHVILLE, TENNESSEE

—

Gift of Ralph E. Becker, 1975

The display manager of Harvey's department store in downtown Nashville, Tennessee, kept this photograph with a newspaper clipping about his humorous poll that, like so many others, failed to predict the outcome of the 1948 presidential contest between Harry S. Truman and Thomas E. Dewey.

The drubbing of Dewey that year famously embarrassed public-opinion pollsters in the world of advertising, who tried to use the presidential election to demonstrate the infallibility of their predictive techniques and models of effect. Though their opinion-sampling techniques were more focused and refined than Harvey's (individuals likely to buy neckwear at a posh department store were more likely to vote Republican, skewing the store's sample), they shared the same flawed results.

FDR's death in 1945 had catapulted Vice President Harry S. Truman to the presidency, and no one gave him much of a chance in 1948. Opinion pollster George Gallup, for example, believed that a Dewey victory was inevitable and missed a critical shift in public opinion toward Truman in the final weeks of the campaign.[11]

The photograph of Harvey's display window was kept as a memento in the same way that newspapers erroneously reporting Dewey's victory were kept. The reverse of the photo carries an undated inscription from Howard L. Fanning, Harvey's display director, who presented it to Bernard V. Somers, the assistant journal clerk of the US Senate, "Compliments of Harveys."

# Bucket used by the
# Eisenhower-Nixon campaign

## NEW YORK, NEW YORK

—

Gift of Ralph E. Becker, 1975

This painted galvanized bucket is believed to have been used on election night in 1952 at Eisenhower-Nixon headquarters in New York City. The bucket held water used to clean and update chalkboard tallies of incoming election returns.

When the returns were tallied, Republican Dwight D. Eisenhower had defeated Democrat Adlai E. Stevenson, winning 55 percent of the popular vote and 442 of 531 Electoral College votes. Soundly defeated, Stevenson lost his home state of Illinois, winning only nine states mostly in the heavily Democratic South.

Throughout the 1950s the Republican party deployed the iconography of housekeeping in the form of mops, brooms, and buckets representing the intent to clean up Washington by purging Democratic Party officeholders dating to the New Deal.[12]

Finely lettered and detailed, this specially painted bucket was created for the Eisenhower-Nixon campaign by a commercial display company. Washington, DC, attorney and collector Ralph E. Becker kept it as a memento and later donated it to the museum as part of an extensive collection of political Americana.

# Kennedy-Nixon television debate chairs

## CHICAGO, ILLINOIS

—

Gift of Frank N. Stanton, 1977

These teak chairs graced the television set of the first of four televised debates between presidential candidates John F. Kennedy and Richard M. Nixon on September 26, 1960. The chairs' sleek, functional design reflected the candidates' forward-looking aspirations as well as those of the broadcast-industry executives who had long hoped to stage such a television meeting. A signal event in the history of television and electoral campaigning, the Kennedy-Nixon debate established new standards and expectations for candidate preparation, performance, and appearance.

The Danish designer Hans J. Wegner had created the chairs as part of a furniture line manufactured by Johannes Hansen in Copenhagen in 1952. Prior to the chairs' appearance in the debate, which was staged at CBS's Chicago affiliate, they furnished the Madison Avenue office of CBS president Frank N. Stanton. After the debate, Stanton had an engraved silver plaque attached to the back of each chair identifying its user. Stanton continued to use and display the chairs in his New York office until he retired from CBS in 1973. He took the chairs with him to his new office as the president of the American Red Cross in Washington, DC, where he invited the Smithsonian to consider the chairs for its collection.[13]

1960

# John F. Kennedy PT-109 tie clip

Gift of Mrs. Evelyn N. Lincoln, 1964

This bronze tie clip's nautical design was modeled after the boat—PT-109—that young Lieutenant John F. Kennedy skippered in the South Pacific during the Second World War. While Kennedy patrolled one night, a Japanese destroyer rammed the boat. The rescue of Kennedy and his marooned crew from a remote and uninhabited island became the stuff of legend. The dramatic story of the rescue, recounted by John Hersey in the *New Yorker*, was reprinted in *Reader's Digest* and widely distributed by Kennedy's congressional campaign in 1946. The tale turned PT-109 into a symbol of virility, perseverance, and courageous derring-do.

During Kennedy's 1960 presidential campaign, a flood of PT boats, from plastic bathtub toys to pin-back buttons, extended to the candidate's personal attire in the form of this PT-109 tie clip. Created for the campaign, the clip became a status symbol worn by family members, the president's inner circle, and a stream of Oval Office visitors, including Benjamin Kevu, a Solomon Islands native who had participated in the future president's South Sea island rescue.

After Kennedy's death in 1963, his longtime secretary, Evelyn Lincoln, cataloged the president's manuscripts, documents, and White House memorabilia, which she later shared with collectors. (Some presidential material of a personal and official nature was reclaimed by the Kennedy family and the National Archives after Lincoln's death in 1995.)[14] Lincoln gave this PT-109 tie clip to Smithsonian curator Herbert R. Collins, who visited her in 1964. Lincoln explained that a supply of the clips had been produced for Kennedy to give away as souvenirs. Five were modeled in gold for him to wear. Despite the cautions of his staff to not distribute the gold ones, he gave them away with the bronze ones.

# *Magnifying glass and chads*

## BROWARD COUNTY, FLORIDA

—

Gift of Robert A. Rosenberg, 2001 and 2004

The presidential contest between George W. Bush and Al Gore came down to Florida in November 2000. As the rest of the nation looked on, four counties began a hand recount of their paper punch-card ballots. The various recounts involved a visual inspection of ballots for discrepancies, as indicated by the punch of a prescored hole through the card. The inadequacies of ballot design, voters' inability to indicate a candidate preference with a clean punch, or both hampered the recount effort that ground into late November until it was halted by the US Supreme Court.

In Broward County, Florida, teams of counters examined each ballot, forwarding cards in need of interpretation to Judge Robert A. Rosenberg. Describing his role as "not unlike that of an umpire at a baseball game," Rosenberg reviewed each card's issues and ruled, where possible, on the voter's intent. Rosenberg, who had astigmatism, found he had to remove his glasses to focus on the incompletely punched holes that resulted in the tiny fragments, known as *chads*, that hung by two or three points from the questionable cards. He asked a clerk for a magnifying glass. Associated Press photographer Alan noticed too, and later that day, Diaz's photo of Rosenberg, holding a ballot in one hand and the glass in the other, became the visual shorthand for this closely fought election, in which each individual vote was crucial.[15]

This is one of two magnifying glasses that Rosenberg used and kept as mementos. A second donation added his business card, stapled to a small plastic bag containing "authentic chads."

AUTHENTIC
CHADS
Broward County
2000 Presidential Election

# ACKNOWLEDGMENTS

In an undertaking with such varied subject matter as this, I became dependent upon the kindness and expertise of others. I am indebted to the museum and library professionals whose collections share similar things, and who made them available to me for the asking: Ann Berry, Pilgrim Hall; Laura B. Simo and Dean Norton, Mount Vernon; Frederick J. Augustyn, Jr., Library of Congress Manuscript Division; Amanda M. Fulcher and Merry Ann Wright, National Society of the Daughters of the American Revolution; Yvonne Carignan, Lida Holland Churchville, Elizabeth Ratigan, Adam Lewis, and Jack Brewer, Kiplinger Research Library, Historical Society of Washington, D.C.; Faye Haskins, Washingtoniana Division, DC Public Library; Katherine A. Cowan, Decker Library, Maryland Institute College of Art; Gavin W. Kleespies and Mark J. Vassar, Cambridge Historical Society; Charles M. Sullivan, Cambridge Historical Commission; Dennis Northcott, Missouri History Museum Archives; Daniel Lewis, Huntington Library; Chris Maiorano and Thayer Eldridge, Plympton Historical Society; Marsha Mullin, The Hermitage; Tom Price, James K. Polk House; Kathy Struss, Dwight D. Eisenhower Presidential Library and Museum; Karie Diethorn, Independence National Historical Park; and Jeanae Biddiscombe, Louisiana State Museum.

My colleagues in the Division of Political History, National Museum of American History, offered encouragement, support, and their special knowledge of collections that enriched my developing study: Harry R. Rubenstein, Barbara Clark Smith, Harry Rand, Lisa Kathleen Graddy, Marilyn Higgins, Debra Hashim, Patricia Mansfield, Sara Murphy, and interns Patrick Loftus, Kasey M. Greer, Paul Roveda, and Emily Cranfill. I have also benefited from conversations about the storied past of the museum's collections and exhibitions with Brian Daniels, Nancy Bercaw, Rayna Green, Richard E. Stamm, Kate Henderson, Jennifer L. Jones, Kathy Golden, David Miller, Craig Orr, Timothy Nolan, Judy Gradwohl, Howard Morrison, Raelene Worthington, Nan Card, Melanie Blanchard, Erin McKeen, Jeanne Benas, Shirley Cherkasky, Barbara J. Coffee, Herbert R. Collins, Keith E. Melder, Edith P. Mayo, Marc Pachter, John L. Gray, Lee Woodman, David Allison, Jim Gardner, Hal Aber, Arthur P. Molella, Bernard Finn, Benjamin W. Lawless, and the late Donald E. Kloster and Silvio A. Bedini. I also benefited from collections visits with Felicia Pickering of the Department of Anthropology, National Museum of Natural History, who graciously showed me the ethnographic specimens collected by John Varden. Ellen Alers and Courtney Esposito lent their expertise in all things Varden at the Smithsonian Institution Archives.

I wish to thank the deep collection and ever helpful librarians of the Smithsonian Institution Libraries: Stephanie Thomas,

Jim Roan, Chris Cotrill, Paul McCutcheon, Trina Brown, Alexia MacClain, Bill Baxter, and Kirsten van der Veen, and especially Wanda West, who often unblocked my overdue interlibrary loan account.

The design and construction of the accompanying exhibition is a credit to the talent and drive of Diane Niedner, Ellen Dorn, Jan Lilja, Catherine Perge, Ann Burrola, Russell Cashdollar, Megan Smith, Beth Richwine, Richard Barden, Karen Garlick, Margaret Grandine, Seth Waite, Peter Albritton, and Omar Wynn. For their kind help in outreach and support I wish to thank Matt MacArthur, Matt Ringelstetter, Rick Luhrs, Barbara Jordan, Robert Gaskill, Doug Womer, Ed Brown, Laura Duff, Valeska Hilbig, and Melinda Machado.

I enjoyed many opportunities to speak about the collection and my developing research. I am indebted to the NMAH Tuesday Colloquium, produced by David Haberstich and Roger Sherman; the museum's Objects Out of Storage series, produced by Bill Yeingst and Kathy Dirks; Thirst DC, produced by Eric Schulze and Kelly Carnes; and especially the Department of American Studies lecture series at the University of Notre Dame, led by Professor Erika Doss.

The clarity of new color photography and scans of archival images is a tribute to photographers Richard W. Strauss and Hugh Talman, archivists Marguerite Roby and Michael Barnes, and to the superb digital-asset management of Alicia M. Cutler.

For kind advice and criticism I wish to thank Rosemary Regan, who edited and commented upon an early draft of the manuscript, and my readers Teresa Barnett, Pamela M. Henson, Liza Kirwin, Robert C. Post, Mary V. Thompson, and Helena E. Wright.

I wish to thank Jennifer Lippert and Sara Stemen of Princeton Architectural Press for their insightful and patient encouragement.

# NOTES

## INTRODUCTION

1. Meredith Arms Bzdak and Douglas Petersen, "Trenton Battle Monument, 1891–1893," in *Public Sculpture in New Jersey: Monuments to Collective Identity* (Piscataway, NJ: Rutgers University Press, 1999), pp. 26–37. The Mount Vernon Ladies' Association received the triumphal arch piece as a donation in 1951.

2. For an overview of the souvenir, see Beverly Gordon, "The Souvenir: Messenger of the Extraordinary," *Journal of Popular Culture* 20 (Winter 1986): 135–46; Steven Lubar and Kathleen M. Kendrick, *Legacies: Collecting America's History at the Smithsonian* (Washington, DC: Smithsonian Institution Press, 2001), pp. 36–41; Rachel P. Maines and James T. Glynn, "Numinous Objects," *The Public Historian* 15 (Winter 1993): 8–25; Teresa Lynn Barnett, "The Nineteenth-Century Relic: A Pre-History of the Historical Artifact" (PhD dissertation, University of California, Los Angeles, 2008), pp. 78–106, cited with the permission of the author. For the souvenir and tourism, see John F. Sears, *Sacred Places: American Tourist Attractions in the Nineteenth Century* (New York: Oxford University Press, 1989), pp. 27–28, 216; G. Evans, "Mementoes to Take Home: The Ancient Trade in Souvenirs," in *In Search of Heritage: As Pilgrim or Tourist?*, ed. J. M. Fladmark (Shaftesbury, UK: Donhead, 1998), pp. 105–26; Michael Hitchcock and Ken Teague, eds., *Souvenirs: The Material Culture of Tourism* (Burlington, VT: Ashgate, 2000); Kristen K. Swanson, "Tourists' and Retailers' Perceptions of Souvenirs," *Journal of Vacation Marketing* 10 (September 2004): 363–77; Dallen J. Timothy, *Shopping Tourism, Retailing, and Leisure* (London and Buffalo, NY: Channel View, 2005), pp. 98–101. For contemporary dilemmas of taking and making, see Eric Lipton and James Glanz, "From the Rubble, Artifacts of Anguish," *New York Times*, January 27, 2002, pp. 1, 16; Mateo Taussig-Rubbo, "Sacred Property: Searching for Value in the 9/11 Rubble," *Buffalo Legal Studies Research Paper No. 2008–24* (May 5, 2009), Social Science Research Network, http://papers.ssrn.com/sol3/papers.cfm?abstract_id=1269533.

3. J. Pollard, "Guide to the National Museum," in *The Washington and Georgetown Directory, Strangers' Guide-Book for Washington, and Congressional and Clerks' Register*, comp. Alfred Hunter (Washington, DC: Kirkwood & McGill, 1853), pp. 45–47; John Varden, *A Guide for Visitors to the National Gallery* (Washington, DC: Polkinhorn's Steam Printing Office, January 1857); Alfred Hunter, *Extraordinary Curiosities in the National Institute, Arranged in the Building Belonging to the Patent Office* (Washington, DC: Alfred Hunter, 1859), p. 31; Douglas E. Evelyn, "The National Gallery at the Patent Office," in *Magnificent Voyagers: The U.S. Exploring Expedition, 1838–1842*, eds. Herman J. Viola and Carolyn Margolis (Washington, DC: Smithsonian Institution Press, 1985), pp. 226–41; Charles J. Robertson, "A Museum of Curiosities," in *Temple of Invention: History of a National Landmark* (London: Scala, 2006), pp. 32–37.

4. Silvio A. Bedini, *Declaration of Independence Desk: Relic of Revolution* (Washington, DC: Smithsonian Institution Press, 1981), pp. 34–36; Harry R. Rubenstein and Barbara Clark Smith, *The Jefferson Bible, Smithsonian Edition: The Life and Morals of Jesus of Nazareth by Thomas Jefferson* (Washington, DC: Smithsonian Books, 2011); Barnett, "The Nineteenth-Century Relic," pp. 78–83.

5. Brooke Hindle, "How Much Is a Piece of the True Cross Worth?" in *Material Culture and the Study of American Life*, ed. Ian M. G. Quimby (New York: W. W. Norton, 1978), p. 20.

6. Jean B. Lee, ed., *Experiencing Mount Vernon: Eyewitness Accounts, 1784–1865* (Charlottesville, VA: University of Virginia Press, 2006), pp. 102–3; 123–26.

7. David Rotenstein, "The gas man's Mount Vernon factory on Capitol Hill," Greater Greater Washington, posted July 19, 2011, http://greatergreaterwashington.org/post/11306/the-gas-mans-mount-vernon-factory-on-capitol-hill/; "Washington Canes," *Kansas Times*, June 26, 1921; Scott E. Casper, *Sarah Johnson's Mount Vernon: The Forgotten History of an American Shrine* (New York: Hill and Wang, 2008), p. 66.

8. Harrison Howell Dodge, *Mount Vernon: Its Owner and Its Story* (Philadelphia: J. B. Lippincott, 1932), pp. 60–61. Elizabeth Bryant Johnston authored the first *Visitors' Guide to Mount Vernon* (Washington, DC: Gibson Brothers, 1876), p. 50. Johnston lived at Mount Vernon to compose her guide and later published descriptions of George Washington portraiture and sculpture. While she was a resident of Mount Vernon, part of the wood flooring was declared unsafe and replaced. Johnston was given original floorboards that she had made into her writing table. Minnie F. Mickey, "Tribute to Miss Elizabeth Bryant Johnston," *Records of the Columbia Historical Society* 11 (1908): 404–6; for additional accounts, see "Mount Vernon in Winter," *New York Times*, February 19, 1893, p. 17; James C. Rees, "Preservation: The Ever Changing Frontier," in *George Washington's Mount Vernon*, ed. Wendell Garrett (New York: Monacelli, 1998), pp. 218–41.

9. Casper, *Sarah Johnson's Mount Vernon*, p. 67.

10. *History of the Great Western Sanitary Fair* (Cincinnati: C. F. Vent, 1864), pp. 360–61.

11. Twain attributed the vandal's failure to the quality of "Egyptian granite that has defied the storms and earthquakes of all time [and] has nothing to fear from the tack-hammers of ignorant excursionists—highwaymen like this specimen." Mark Twain, *The Innocents Abroad* (Hartford, CT: American Publishing Company, 1869), pp. 612, 630.

12. "Relic-Hunting," *The American Architect and Building News*, August 20, 1881, p. 90, reprinted from *New York Times*.

13. "The Dire Souvenir Mania," from *New York Herald*, reprinted in *Washington Post*, August 24, 1911, p. 6.

14. "The Stream of Centennial Sight-Seers Exploring the Capital," *Chicago Daily Tribune*, October 8, 1876, p. 8; "Damage to a Work of Art," *Washington Post*, October 6, 1899, p. 7; Frank G. Carpenter, "Washington Gossip," *Los Angeles Times*, May 24, 1887, p. 9.

15. "Relic Hunters Haunt the White House," *New York Times*, June 23, 1902, p. 3; "Vandals Barred at White House," *Chicago Tribune*, July 14, 1902, p. 2.

16. "Profits in Souvenirs," *Washington Post*, September 27, 1903, p. E3.

17. Heather Ewing, *The Lost World of James Smithson: Science, Revolution, and the Birth of the Smithsonian Institution* (New York: Bloomsbury, 2007); William L. Bird, Jr., "A Suggestion Concerning James Smithson's Concept of 'Increase and Diffusion,'" *Technology and Culture* 24 (April 1983): 246–55; Cyrus Adler, "The Relation of Richard Rush to the Smithsonian Institution," *Smithsonian Institution Miscellaneous Collections* 52 (1910): 235–51.

18. Sec. 6 and Sec. 7, "An Act to Establish the 'Smithsonian Institution' for the Increase and Diffusion of Knowledge Among Men" [as finally adopted and made into law, August 10, 1846], 29th Congress, 1st Session, Smithsonian Institution Libraries, http://www.sil.si.edu/Exhibitions/ Smithson-to-Smithsonian/1846act.htm; Hunter Dupree, *Science and the Federal Government: A History of Policies and Activities to 1940* (Cambridge, MA: Belknap, 1957), pp. 66–90.

19. Wilcomb E. Washburn, "Joseph Henry's Conception of the Purpose of the Smithsonian Institution," in *A Cabinet of Curiosities: Five Episodes in the Evolution of American Museums*, Whitfield J. Bell, Jr., et al. (Charlottesville, VA: University Press of Virginia, 1967), pp. 106–66; Bird, "A Suggestion Concerning James Smithson's Concept of 'Increase and Diffusion'"; Sally Gregory Kohlstedt, *The Formation of the American Scientific Community: The American Association for the Advancement of Science 1848–60* (Urbana, IL: University of Illinois Press, 1976), p. 18; George H. Daniels, "The Process of Professionalization in American Science: The Emergent Period, 1820–1860," *Isis* 58 (Summer 1967): 151–66. For examples of Henry's "not educational" statements, see *Third Annual Report of the Board of Regents of the Smithsonian Institution, to the Senate and House of Representatives, Showing the Operations, Expenditures, and Condition of the Institution During the Year 1848* (Washington, DC: Tippin & Streeper, Printers, 1849), p. 18; *Smithsonian Institution Miscellaneous Collections* (Washington, DC: Smithsonian Institution, 1887), 30: 286. *Publishers Weekly* claimed that there was no free distribution of Smithsonian publications to individuals. "Smithsonian Institution Publications," *Publishers Weekly* 29 (March 6, 1886): 333.

20. Henry to Asa Gray, April 6, 1857, Gray Herbarium, Harvard University, cited in Kenneth Hafertepe, *America's Castle: The Evolution of the Smithsonian Building and Its Institution, 1840–1878* (Washington, DC: Smithsonian Institution Press, 1984), p. 129.

21. The collections transferred were those gathered by US Navy and Army officers attached to exploring expeditions to the South Pacific and the western territories and boundary and railroad surveying parties. Catalog in the Department of Anthropology, National Museum of Natural History, Suitland, Maryland.

22. Varden often described the history of his collection. Varden, copy fragment, May 16, 1853, folder 14, box 10, outgoing correspondence, 1851–1853, National Institute Records 1839–1863, RG 7058, Smithsonian Institution Archives (hereafter SIA); John C. Ewers, "A Century of American Indian Exhibits in the Smithsonian Institution," in *Annual Report of the Board of Regents of the Smithsonian Institution Publication 4354 Showing the Operations, Expenditures, and condition of the Institution for the Year Ended June 30, 1958* (Washington, DC: United States Government Printing Office, 1959), pp. 513–25; Vladimir Clain-Stefanelli, *History of the National Numismatic Collections, Contributions from the Museum of History and Technology: Paper 31, Bulletin 229* (Washington, DC: Government Printing Office, 1970), pp. 142–43; Evelyn, "The National Gallery at the Patent Office"; William Stanton, *The Great United States Exploring Expedition of 1838–1842* (Berkeley, CA: University of California Press, 1975), pp. 294–359; Pamela M. Henson, "A National Science and a National Museum," in *Museums and Other Institutions of Natural History*, ed. Alan E. Leviton and Michael L. Aldrich (San Francisco: California Academy of Sciences, 2004), pp. 34–57. For a thumbnail biography of Varden, see Richard E. Stamm, *The Castle: An Illustrated History of the Smithsonian Building* (Washington, DC: Smithsonian Books, 2012), p. 71.

23. "Convention of Soldiers of the War of 1812," *Baltimore Sun*, January 10, 1856, p. 1; "Survivors of the Soldiers of the War of 1812," *Daily National Intelligencer* [hereafter *DNI*], June 19, 1857; "Death of an Old Veteran," *Baltimore Sun*, February 13, 1865, p. 1.

24. John S. Kendall, *The Golden Age of the New Orleans Theater* (Baton Rouge: Louisiana State University Press, 1952), p. 42.

25. Cowell wrote, "On the afternoon of the first performance I got a note from John Quincy Adams, then the President, requiring a certain box for that evening, directed to '*Mr. Manager of the Theatre*'; and I sent a reply, regretting that he couldn't have it

till five nights afterward, directed to '*Mr. Manager of the United States*.' I was afterward told that the kind old man was highly amused by the response." Joe Cowell, *Thirty Years Passed Among the Players in England and America* (New York: Harper & Bros., 1844), pp. 82–83.

26. Entries for October 31, 1829; November 6, 1829; and January 1, 1830, Varden diaries, John Varden papers, 1829–1863, folder 2, box 1, RG 7063, SIA.

27. Brigham, *Public Culture in the Early Republic*; Gary Kulik, "Designing the Past: History-Museum Exhibitions from Peale to the Present," in *History Museums in the United States: A Critical Assessment*, ed. Warren Leon and Roy Rosenzweig (Urbana, IL: University of Illinois Press, 1989), pp. 2–37; Wilcomb E. Washburn, "The Influence of the Smithsonian Institution on Intellectual Life in Mid-Nineteenth Century Washington," *Records of the Columbian Historical Society of Washington, DC* 63/65: 96–121; Whitfield J. Bell, Jr., describes the duties of a curator: keeping a book of donors and objects received by the American Philosophical Society (p. 4) in "The Cabinet of the American Philosophical Society," in *A Cabinet of Curiosities*, Bell et al. (Charlottesville, VA: University Press of Virginia, 1967), pp. 1–34.

28. Advertisement, "Washington Museum," *DNI*, May 31, 1836; "Washington Museum," *DNI*, July 4, 1836; entry for June 1, 1836, Varden diaries, SIA.

29. A Visitor, "Communications," *DNI*, July 22, 1836.

30. Advertisement, "To Carpenters," *DNI*, September 29, 1835; "National Theatre," *DNI*, December 9, 1835; playbills, *DNI*, December 5, 1836; December 14, 1836; December 22, 1836; February 2, 1837; February 20, 1837.

31. Kendall, *The Golden Age of the New Orleans Theater*, p. 162.

32. *DNI*, June 17, 1839.

33. Peter Benes, "'A few monstrous great snakes': Daniel Bowen and the Columbian Museum, 1789–1816," in *New England Collectors and Collections*, ed. Benes (Boston: Boston University, 2006), pp. 22–39.

34. "C. Boyle announces the organization of a "National Museum," *DNI*, April 21, 1809; announcement of the opening of J. Griffith's "Museum of Natural and Artificial Curiosities," *DNI*, October 11, 1823 and "Loss of the Museum," *DNI*, July 26, 1825; classified ad, "National Museum and Gallery of Fine Arts," *DNI*, November 20, 1830.

35. Varden pledged that all donations "shall not be removed from the city during the lifetime of the proprietor." Varden, "Washington Museum," *DNI*, August 22, 1836.

36. Ewers, "A Century of American Indian Exhibits in the Smithsonian Institution." Varden may have taken the phrase from the Peales. On Peale's and others' description of the museum and even the circus as a "rational entertainment" and "rational amusement" in the name of socially beneficial leisure, see David R. Brigham, *Public Culture in the Early Republic: Peale's Museum and Its Audience* (Washington, DC: Smithsonian Institution Press, 1995), pp. 20–21; for an example of Varden's early advertisements beyond the prevalent *Daily National Intelligencer*, see "Washington Museum," *Globe* (Washington, DC), August 21, 1837.

37. Varden offered annual subscriptions to individuals at five dollars or families at ten dollars. In 1840 he recorded fifty-eight subscriptions from thirty-eight families and twenty individuals. Varden, "Subscriptions to the Washington Museum for the Year 1840 Beginning Jan 1st," William Jones Rhees papers, RH 563, Huntington Library, Pasadena, CA.

38. Advertisement, "Washington Museum," *DNI*, January 21, 1840; February 10, 1840; June 15, 1840.

39. "Grand Exhibitions," *DNI*, February 10, 1840.

40. "Board of Common Council, Monday, February 10, 1840," *DNI*, February 12, 1840; February 26, 1840.

41. *DNI*, March 4, 1840.

42. Though neither the mummies nor the source of Varden's purchase can be located today, circumstantial evidence points to Ethan Allen Greenwood, a collector and exhibitor who sold two Egyptian mummies in the 1830s. Georgia F. Barnhill, "Ethan Allen Greenwood: Museum Collector and Proprietor," in *New England Collectors and Collections*, ed. Benes, pp. 42–52.

43. *DNI*, July 21, 1840; September 9, 1840; December 16, 1840; February 12, 1841.

44. Varden, May 16, 1853, National Institute Records, folder 14, box 10, SIA; Ewers, "A Century of American Indian Exhibits in the Smithsonian Institution"; Evelyn, "The National Gallery at the Patent Office."

45. Ewers, "A Century of American Indian Exhibits in the Smithsonian Institution"; Evelyn, "The National Gallery at the Patent Office"; marriage record, John Varden-Alice Ptolma, Baltimore, Maryland, December 12, 1841, "Maryland Marriages, 1655–1850," AncestryLibrary.com.

46. Pollard, "Guide to the National Museum," in *The Washington and Georgetown Directory*, comp. Hunter; Varden, *A Guide for Visitors to the National Gallery*; Robertson, "A Museum of Curiosities."

47. On the Franklin press, see "Correspondence of the Baltimore Sun," *Baltimore Sun*, February 24, 1845, p. 4. Henry wrote to Varden at the Patent Office in 1847 and urged him to gather and preserve Smithson's personal papers and effects, which had been collected for the government by the envoy Richard Rush in 1838. Smithson's papers were transferred to the Smithsonian in 1850 at Henry's request. Henry to Varden, March 29, 1847, in Marc Rothenberg, ed., *The Papers of Joseph Henry* (Washington, DC: Smithsonian Institution Press, 1996), 7: 68–69; from Joseph Henry, "receipt of papers from James Smithson and other," April 9, 1850, RG 59, SD Reg. of LR (1850), Row 11, National Archives and Records Administration.

48. "Correspondence of the Baltimore Sun," *Baltimore Sun*, March 1, 1853, p. 4 and April 23, 1853, p. 4; Varden, "Copy of letter to Joshua Vansant, President of the Maryland Institute," September 25, 1855, Records of the National Institute, box 10, folder 15, RU 7058, SIA; Helena E. Wright, *The First Smithsonian Collection: An Account of the European Engravings of George Perkins Marsh and the Reception of Prints in Nineteenth-Century America* (forthcoming).

49. George Brown Goode, "The Genesis of the United States National Museum," in *A Memorial of George Brown Goode, Together with a Selection of His Papers on Museums and on the History of Science in America* (Washington, DC:

Government Printing Office, 1901), pp. 83–191; on the museum's name, see p. 159.

50. Kathleen W. Dorman, "'Interruptions and Embarrassments': The Smithsonian Institution during the Civil War," Joseph Henry Papers Project, Smithsonian Institution Archives, http://siarchives.si.edu/history/jhp/Civilwar.htm.

51. Varden concluded, "So that you see that the Institution [sic] is dead & they want to burry [sic] what is left in the Smithsonian Institution." Varden to Spencer Fullerton Baird, September 14, 1861, Spencer Fullerton Baird Papers, 1833–1889, box 35, folder 5: Varden, John, 1860–1862, RU 7002, SIA; Sally Gregory Kohlstedt, "A Step Toward Scientific Self-Identity in the United States: The Failure of the National Institute, 1844," Isis 62 (Autumn 1971): 339–62.

52. The United States Sanitary Commission described itself as "the great artery which bears the people's love to the people's army." The United States Sanitary Commission: A Sketch of Its Purposes and Its Work (Boston: Little, Brown, 1863), p. 1; Beverly Gordon, Bazaars and Fair Ladies: The History of the American Fundraising Fair (Knoxville, TN: University of Tennessee Press, 1998), pp. 60–86; Judith Ann Giesberg, Civil War Sisterhood: The U.S. Sanitary Commission and Women's Politics in Transition (Boston: Northeastern University Press, 2000).

53. Department of Arms and Trophies, Metropolitan Fair, Catalogue of the Museum of Flags, Trophies and Relics Relating to the Revolution, the War of 1812, the Mexican War, and the Present Rebellion (New York: Charles O. Jones, 1864), pp. 102–4; "The Metropolitan Fair," New York Times, April 4, 1864, p. 1; A Record of the Metropolitan Fair in Aid of the United States Sanitary Commission, Held at New York, in April 1864 (New York: Hurd and Houghton, 1867), p. 36. On relic room displays, see Gordon, Bazaars and Fair Ladies; William Y. Thompson, "Sanitary Fairs of the Civil War," Civil War History 4 (March 1958): 51–67; for photographs, see William C. Davis, ed., The Image of War, 1861–1865, Vol. 1: Shadows of the Storm (Garden City, NY: Doubleday, 1981), pp. 400–4; Stephen W. Sylvia and Michael J. O'Donnell, The Illustrated History of American Civil War Relics (Orange, VA: Moss, 1985), pp. 58–59.

54. The Daily National Intelligencer reported that Varden had sought to preserve the property during the fire. "Another Old Citizen Gone," DNI, February 11, 1865. Joseph Henry wrote that Varden had been at home "unwell" for some time and visited the scene of the fire the following day, "looking very badly," suggesting that Varden's exposure to the damage hastened his demise. Henry, diary entry, February 12, 1865, desk diary, 1849–1866, folder 6: 1865, SIA; Henry to John Peter Lesley, February 11, 1865, and Nancy Clarke Fowler Bache, February 25, 1865, in Rothenberg, ed., The Papers of Joseph Henry, Volume 10, pp. 472, 478; Stamm, The Castle, pp. 90–93.

55. "Report of the Special Committee of the Board of Regents of the Smithsonian Institution Relative to the Fire," in The Smithsonian Institution: Documents Relative to Its Origin and History, ed. William J. Rhees (Washington, DC: Smithsonian Institution, 1879), pp. 686–89; Hafertepe, America's Castle, pp. 132–36. Smithson's relics were placed on display in the Regent's Room in 1857. Stamm, The Castle, pp. 133–35.

56. The boxed material was not itemized. Joseph Henry to Mrs. John Varden, October 31, 1865, box 1, v. 2, p. 67, micro #3, RU 33, SIA; Joseph Henry to R. T. Campbell, November 2, 1867, box 6, v. 8, p. 132, micro reel #9, RU 33, SIA; Joseph Henry to Mrs. J. Varden, May 14, 1869, box 6, v. 14, pp. 532–33, micro #21, RU 33, SIA.

57. Ewers, "A Century of American Indian Exhibits in the Smithsonian Institution"; Clain-Stefanelli, History of the National Numismatic Collections; William B. Dinsmoor, "Early American Studies of Mediterranean Archaeology," Proceedings of the American Philosophical Society 87 (July 14, 1943): 70–104 (see p. 79); W. A. Hart, "Early Nineteenth-Century Chiefs' Horns from Coastal Liberia," African Arts 32 (Autumn 1999): 62–67 +96 (see p. 64); Wright, The First Smithsonian Collection; Philip Kopper, America's National Gallery of Art: A Gift to the Nation (New York: Harry N. Abrams, 1991), pp. 27, 28, 30, 35; Richard Rathbun, The National Gallery of Art: Department of Fine Arts of the National Museum (Washington, DC: Government Printing Office, 1909), pp. 30–31.

58. Henry, February 12, 1865, desk diary, 1849–1866, folder 6: 1865, SIA; Nathan Reingold, "The New York State Roots of Joseph Henry's National Career," New York History 54 (1973): 132–44.

59. E. F. Rivinus and E. M. Youssef, Spencer Baird of the Smithsonian (Washington, DC: Smithsonian Institution Press, 1992), p. 71; William Healey Dall, Spencer Fullerton Baird: A Biography (Philadelphia: J. B. Lippincott, 1915), pp. 211–13, 235; Ellis L. Yochelson, "More than 150 years of Administrative Ups and Downs for Natural History in Washington," in Museums and Other Institutions of Natural History, ed. Alan E. Leviton and Michael L. Aldrich (San Francisco: California Academy of Sciences, 2004), pp. 113–76; Pamela M. Henson, "Baird as Assistant Secretary and the Growth of a Dream," Smithsonian Institution Archives, http://siarchives.si.edu/history/exhibits/baird/bairdc.htm.

60. George Brown Goode, "Report of the Assistant Director of the United States National Museum for the Year 1881," March 1, 1882, p. 89. Goode itemized and described the similarities and differences of fairs and museums. Goode, "The Relationships and Responsibilities of Museums," Science 2 (1895): 197–209, in Museum Origins: Readings in Early Museum History & Philosophy, eds. Hugh H. Genoways and Mary Anne Andrei (Walnut Creek, CA: Left Coast, 2008), pp. 111–24.

61. See the essays by Claudine Klose; Robert C. Post; Craddock R. Goins, Jr.; Donald E. Kloster; Harold D. Langley; Philip K. Lundeberg; and Deborah J. Warner, "The Government Building," in Post, ed., 1876: A Centennial Exhibition (Washington, DC: National Museum of History and Technology, Smithsonian Institution, 1976), pp. 74–95.

62. Sally Gregory Kohlstedt, "History in a Natural History Museum: George Brown Goode and the Smithsonian Institution," The Public Historian 10 (Spring 1988): 7–26.

63. "For the purchase of relics of George Washington from the Lewis family," US Statute, Vol. 20, p. 218; Sundry Civil Appropriation Act of June 30, 1878, for fiscal year ending June 30, 1879; Theodore T. Belote, Descriptive Catalog of the Washington Relics in the United States National Museum

(Washington, DC: Government Printing Office, 1915), pp. 1–2. Belote's catalog drew heavily upon the catalog of Washington relics compiled by Elizabeth Bryant Johnston.

64. Gary Kulik notes that Goode's taxonomy paid little attention to history as any other than a "residual category." Kulik, "Designing the Past: History-Museum Exhibitions from Peale to the Present," in *History Museums in the United States: A Critical Assessment*, ed. Leon and Rosenzweig, pp. 2–37; George Brown Goode, *Report of the United States National Museum* (1881); Goode, "Museum-History and Museums of History, A Paper Read Before the American Historical Association, in Washington City, December 26–28, 1888," in *A Memorial of George Brown Goode*, pp. 65–81; Sally Gregory Kohlstedt, "'Thoughts in Things': Modernity, History, North American Museums," Isis 96 (2005): 586–601; Miriam R. Levin, "Museums and Democratic Order," *Wilson Quarterly* 26 (Winter 2002): 52–65; G. Carroll Lindsay, "George Brown Goode," in *Keepers of the Past*, ed. Clifford L. Lord (Chapel Hill, NC: University of North Carolina Press, 1965), pp. 127–40; "Tour the U.S. National Museum in 1886," Smithsonian Institution Archives, http://siarchives.si.edu/history/exhibits/tour-us-national-museum-1886.

65. C. H. Koster to Spencer F. Baird, December 6, 1884, Unexcelled Fireworks Company, acc. 15386; playing cards, Beckwith, acc. 21245, cat. 4732; buttons, acc. 37407, cats. 209184–20989, Division of Political History, National Museum of American History (hereafter DPH/NMAH).

66. Karal Ann Marling, *George Washington Slept Here: Colonial Revivals and American Culture, 1876–1986* (Cambridge, MA: Harvard University Press, 1988), p. 39; Peggy Anderson, *The Daughters: An Unconventional Look at America's Fan Club—The DAR* (New York: St. Martin's Press, 1974), p. 69; Elisabeth Donaghy Garrett, *The Arts of Independence: The DAR Museum Collection* (Washington, DC: The National Society, Daughters of the American Revolution, 1985), p. 12.

67. David D. Van Tassel, "From Learned Society to Professional Organization: The American Historical Association, 1884–1900," *American Historical Review* 89 (October 1984): 929–56.

68. Goode documented the presence of his forebears in colonial Virginia. Goode, *Virginia Cousins: A Study of the Ancestry and Posterity of John Goode of Whitby, A Virginia Colonist of the Seventeenth Century* (Richmond, VA: J. W. Randolph & English, 1887).

69. Historical accounts of the museum's partnership with the AHA emphasize the publication of the organization's annual reports, not collecting activities. Arthur S. Link, "The American Historical Association, 1884–1984: Retrospect and Prospect," *American Historical Review* 90 (February 1985): 1–17; Van Tassel, "From Learned Society to Professional Organization," pp. 929–56. One historian pronounced the AHA's manuscript collection "completely useless." Dallas D. Irvine, "The Genesis of the Official Records," *Mississippi Valley Historical Review* 24 (September 1937): 221–29.

70. Clark to H. B. Adams, March 30, 1888 and Clark to file, April 9, 1888, letter book, National Numismatic Collection, NMAH.

71. "Paul Edmond Chouteau Beckwith" and "Alonzo Howard Clark," *Register of the Society of Colonial Wars in the District of Columbia* (Washington, DC: privately printed, 1904), pp. 38, 58; "Funeral of P. E. Beckwith," *Washington Post*, June 30, 1907, p. 12. Pictured in his Minuteman uniform, Beckwith participated in a national newspaper advertising campaign for a cough-syrup manufacturer. For one graphic example among many, see "For Coughs and Colds, Col. Beckwith of Washington Recommends Pe-ru-na," *Colorado Springs Gazette*, January 23, 1904, p. 3.

72. Martha Strayer, *The D.A.R.: An Informal History* (Washington, DC: Public Affairs Press, 1958), pp. 1–6; "With the Spirit of '76: Sons of Revolutionary Soldiers Have Banded Themselves Together," *Washington Post*, July 5, 1890, p. 7; Mary S. Lockwood, "Women Worthy of Honor: The Patriotic Spirit of '76. Something for the Sons of the Revolution to Read—Hannah Thurston Arnett," *Washington Post*, July 13, 1890, p. 12.

73. Garrett, *The Arts of Independence*, pp. 7–12.

74. Goode filed a patent application August 3, 1891, serial no. 401584; design no. 21,053, dated September 22, 1891. On the DAR-Smithsonian relationship, see "Spinning Wheel of D.A.R. Significance," *Daughters of the American Revolution Magazine* LXII (May 1928): 273; Lark L. Toms, "The Smithsonian—'Ward' of the Federal Government," *Daughters of the American Revolution Magazine* LXVII (March 1933): 134–39; Mrs. Charles H. Danforth, "The Smithsonian Institution and the D.A.R.," *The Daughters of the American Revolution Magazine* 85 (July 1951): 551–57, 587; Carl F. Bessent, "The SAR and DAR Working Together," in *Centennial History of the National Society of the Sons of the American Revolution, 1889–1989*, ed. Bessent (Paducah, KY: Turner, 1991), pp. 22–23.

75. Pamela M. Henson, "'Objects of Curious Research': The History of Science and Technology at the Smithsonian," *Isis* 90: S249–S269.

76. A. Howard Clark, "What the United States Government Has Done for History," *Annual Report of the American Historical Association, 1894* (Washington, D.C, 1895), p. 549. Irvine, "The Genesis of the Official Records."

77. Describing the antiquarian basis of American historical societies, Jameson noted, "Not only was it of a more scientific character than most of what had preceded it, but it was of peculiar value as establishing a certain tendency in our historical work; a tendency, namely, to make the publication of materials as much an object of the historical scholar's care as the publication of results. The idea has, to be sure, been slow in taking root." J. Franklin Jameson, *The History of Historical Writing in America* (Boston: Houghton, Mifflin, 1891), p. 88, cited in Van Tassel, "From Learned Society to Professional Organization." Anecdotal evidence from an undated talk that Goode gave to the DAR suggests that he never believed that the reach of the DAR's museum, as yet unrealized, would be any other than local in scope. Speech cards attributed to George Brown Goode, National Numismatic Collection, NMAH. Thanks to Nancy Bercaw for bringing them to my attention.

78. Clark, "Report for 1894," folder: Section of Historical Collections 1893–94; "1896," folder: Section of Historical Collections 1895–96, box 2, RG 158, United States National Museum, Curators' Annual Reports, 1881–1964, SIA.

79. "G. Brown Goode Dead," *Washington Post* (September 7, 1896), p. 1; Theodore Gill, "George Brown Goode," *Science* 4 (November 6, 1886): 661–68; "Sketch of George Brown Goode," *Appleton's Popular Science Monthly* (January 1, 1897), p. 50+.

80. *Ibid.*; Goode to Mary Sawyer Foote (member of the Revolutionary Relics Committee), July 31, 1896, and Foote's account of her visit to see the empty cases cleared by Goode, November 5, 1896, *American Monthly Magazine* 10 (January–June 1997): 100. On the adjacent Copp Collection of New England household effects and Goode's plan, see Briann G. Greenfield, *Out of the Attic: Inventing Antiques in Twentieth-Century New England* (Amherst, MA: University of Massachusetts Press, 2009), pp. 174–77.

81. "Col. Beckwith's Eyes Fail," *Washington Post*, February 11, 1906, p. 6; "Funeral of P. E. Beckwith," *Washington Post*, June 30, 1907, p. 12; "Curator A. Howard Clark, Native of Boston, Dead," *Boston Daily Globe*, January 1, 1919, p. 9.

82. Eleanor Holmes Lindsay (Chairman), *List of Relics Deposited in the Smithsonian Institution by the Revolutionary Relics Committee of the Daughters of the American Revolution* (Washington, DC: Daughters of the American Revolution, 1903). Data from the card catalog of the Division of Political History indicates that between 1897 and 1924, some 265 objects in 46 transactions were deposited by DAR members and cataloged as loans by the museum.

83. Mrs. Joseph Rucker Lamar, *A History of the National Society of the Colonial Dames of America, from 1891 to 1933* (Atlanta, GA: Walter W. Brown, 1934), pp. 232–33.

84. Ellis L. Yochelson, The National Museum of Natural History: *75 Years in the Natural History Building* (Washington, DC: Smithsonian Institution Press, 1990).

85. "Theo. Belote: Was Curator of History," *Washington Post*, December 4, 1953; Belote, *Descriptive Catalog of the Washington Relics in the United States National Museum* (1915); "The War Collection of the United States National Museum," *Daughters of the American Revolution Magazine* 53 (February 1919): 63–78.

86. "European Upheaval Has Molded Late Art, Richards Says," *Washington Post*, May 13, 1924, p. 7; "Arts and Artists of the Capital," *Washington Post*, May 11, 1924, p. A4; Theodore T. Belote, "The Field of the Historical Museum," *Museum Work* 8 (May–June 1925): 9–16.

87. Belote, "The Field of the Historical Museum," 9–16; Arthur C. Parker, "Unhistorical Museums," *Museum Work* 6 (January–February 1924): 155–58.

88. Lonn Taylor, Kathleen M. Kendrick, and Jeffrey L. Brodie, The Star-Spangled Banner: *The Making of an American Icon* (New York: Smithsonian Books, 2008), pp. 109–11.

89. Theresa Lynn Barnett concludes that "the relic had simply ceased to mean at all." Barnett, "The Nineteenth-Century Relic," p. 297.

90. Theodore T. Belote, "History Section of the Smithsonian Institution's New Index Exhibit," *Scientific Monthly* 53 (September 1941): 287–89.

91. Peggy Thompson, "The Dust-Spangled Banner," *Washington Post*, June 18, 1982, p. W37.

92. Memorandum, "Unfinished Business," Richard H. Howland to Dr. Washburn, November 3, 1964, acc. file 70138, Office of the Registrar, NMAH.

93. Wilcomb E. Washburn, "Manuscripts and Manufacts," *American Archivist* 27 (April 1964): 245–50; Bernard Mergen, "Wilcomb E. Washburn, 1925–1997," *Washington History* 9 (Spring/Summer 1997): 71–72.

94. Michael Kernan, "Strange Items from the 'Nation's Attic,'" *Washington Post*, August 8, 1980, p. C10; Michael Killian, "Nation's Attic on Display in Washington," *Chicago Tribune*, April 27, 1980, p. K3.

CHAPTER ONE

1. John McPhee, "Travels of the Rock," in *The Princeton Anthology of Writing: Favorite Pieces by the Ferris/McGraw Writers at Princeton University*, ed. John McPhee and Carol Rigolot (Princeton, NJ: Princeton University Press, 2001), accessed from Princeton University Press website, http://press.princeton.edu/chapters/s5_7108.html; William Seelye, *Memory's Nation: The Place of Plymouth Rock* (Chapel Hill: University of North Carolina Press, 1998).

2. Charlene Mires, *Independence Hall in American Memory* (Philadelphia: University of Pennsylvania Press, 2002), especially pp. 121–34; John C. Milley, ed., *Treasures of Independence: Independence National Historical Park and Its Collections* (New York: Mayflower Books, 1980), pp. 11–25; Edward M. Riley, *Independence National Historical Park, Philadelphia, PA*, Historical Handbook Series 17 (Washington, DC: National Park Service, 1954, revised 1956); Gary B. Nash, *Landmarks of the American Revolution* (New York: Oxford University Press, 2003), pp. 21–34; Gary B. Nash, *The Liberty Bell* (New Haven, CT: Yale University Press, 2011); on the National Museum, see Frank M. Etting, *An Historical Account of the Old State House of Pennsylvania* (Boston: James R. Osgood, 1876), pp. 164–89 and Edward M. Riley, "The Independence Hall Group," *Transactions of the American Philosophical Society* 43 (1953): 7–42, especially p. 39; Dennis C. Kurjack, "Evolution of a Shrine," *Pennsylvania History* 21 (July 1954): 193–200, on Etting, pp. 198–99.

3. Robert F. Trent, "The Charter Oak Artifacts," *Connecticut Historical Society Bulletin* 49 (1984): 125–57; William N. Hosley, "The Romance of a Relic: Sam Colt's Charter Oak Furniture," *Folk Art* 21 (Fall 1996): 49–55; Charles Edgar Randall and Henry Clepper, *Famous and Historic Trees* (Washington, DC: American Forestry Association, 1976), pp. 4, 6.

4. Edward L. Kappol, Jr., Alice Levi Duncan, Bara Levin, and Leslie Weckstein, *Images of Liberty: Models and Reductions of the Statue of Liberty, 1867–1917* (New York: Christie, Manson & Woods, 1985), pp. 1–3, 28–31; "American Committee Model," The Statue of Liberty Club, http://www.statueoflibertyclub.com/collectibles/acm.html; Wilton S. Dillon, "The Ultimate Gift," in *The Statue of Liberty Revisited*, ed. Dillon and Neil G. Kotler, (Washington, DC: Smithsonian Institution Press, 1994), pp. 135–57.

5. "Crowds Hear Case of Women Against Administration," *The Suffragist* 5 (December 15, 1917): 7; "97 'Suff' Pickets to Get Prison Pins," *Washington Post*, December 2, 1917;

"Pickets to Carry Banners," *Washington Post*, December 6, 1917, p. 9; for an example of Pankhurst's brooch, see National Women's History Museum, http://www.nwhm.org/online-exhibits/votesforwomen/tour_02-02t.html. Doris Stevens pictured the iconic pin on the title page of her history of the suffrage campaign, *Jailed for Freedom* (New York: Boni and Liveright, 1920) and described the award ceremony, pp. 245–47; Linda G. Ford, *Iron-Jawed Angels: The Suffrage Militancy of the National Woman's Party, 1912–1920* (Lanham, MD: University Press of America, 1991), pp. 99, 197–223.

CHAPTER TWO

1. Dodge, *Mount Vernon: Its Owner and Its Story*, pp. 184–85; William Strickland, *Tomb of Washington at Mount Vernon* (Philadelphia: Carey and Hart, 1840), p. 37; Jared Sparks noted that the coffin was lead lined. Jared Sparks, *The Writings of Washington* (Boston: American Stationers' Company, 1837), 1: 561; Robert L. Madison, *Walking with Washington: Walking Tours of Alexandria, Virginia* (Baltimore, MD: Gateway Press, 2003), p. 75; Leverett Saltonstall to Mary Saltonstall, February 20, 1825, in *The Papers of Leverett Saltonstall, 1816–1845*, ed. Robert L. Moody (Boston: Massachusetts Historical Society, 1978), 1: 152–53; Leverett Saltonstall to Leverett Saltonstall, Jr., May 16, 1840, 2: 295–96; Leverett Saltonstall to Anne E. Saltonstall, July 5, 1840, 3: 5–6.

2. James Crutchett, "Appeal of James Crutchett to the Government of the United States for Property They Forcibly Seized and Destroyed" (September 27, 1861), cited in Rotenstein, "The gas man's Mount Vernon factory on Capitol Hill"; Robert Hershman, "Gas in Washington," *Records of the Columbia Historical Society* 50 (1948/1950): 137–57; "When Washington Was Younger—No. 191," *Washington Post*, February 11, 1932, p. 17; "Mementoes of Mount Vernon," *The Country Gentleman*, February 5, 1857, p. 9; "Death of Captain Crutchett," *Washington Post*, May 1, 1889, p. 3.

3. "Washington Monument: The Highest Structure of Human Hands Completed Yesterday," *Washington Post*, December 7, 1884, p. 1; Robert Belmont Freeman, "Design Proposals for the Washington Monument," *Records of the Columbia Historical Society* 49 (1973/1974): 151–86; Frederick L. Harvey, *History of the Washington National Monument and of the Washington National Monument Society* (Washington, DC: Norman T. Elliott, 1902), pp. 44–47, 98–99, 103, 108; "'Monument' McLaughlin's Appointment," *Washington Post*, January 19, 1894, p. 5; Frank Freidel and Lonnelle Aikman, *George Washington: Man and Monument* (Washington, DC: Washington National Monument Association, 1988). Toner was eulogized along with George Browne Goode at the annual meeting of the American Historical Association in 1896. "Men Who Make History," *New York Times*, December 30, 1896, p. 2.

4. The brick is inscribed: "Brick collected by myself Sept. 14, 1894 from the debris on the place at Wakefield—Westmoreland Co. Va. Where the house stood in which George Washington was born Feb. 22, 17— [signed] John Heltz." "Built by Women: Monument to the Mother of Washington," *Washington Post*, May 11, 1894, p. 1; Marie Mattingly, "Wakefield in Decay," *Washington Post*, July 28, 1901, p. 13; Evelyn Carpenter,

"Mr. and Mrs. Washington," *Washington Post*, May 25, 1930, p. JP2; Seth Bruggeman, *Here, George Washington Was Born: Memory, Material Culture, and the Public History of a National Monument* (Athens, GA: University of Georgia Press, 2008); Joshua Ruff, "George Washington Birthplace National Monument: Provenance of a Colonial Revival Commemorative Landscape," in *Re-creating the American Past: Essays on the Colonial Revival*, ed. Richard Guy Wilson, Shaun Eyring, and Kenny Marotta (Charlottesville, VA: University of Virginia Press, 2006); J. Paul Hudson, *George Washington Birthplace: National Monument in Virginia*, Historical Handbook Series 26 (Washington, DC: National Park Service, 1958).

5. Edgar Ewing Brandon, ed., *Lafayette, Guest of the Nation: A Contemporary Account of the "Triumphal Tour" of General Lafayette through the United States in 1824–1825 as Reported by the Local Newspapers*, 3 vols. (Oxford, OH: Oxford Historical Press, 1950), p. 123; Lee, ed., *Experiencing Mount Vernon*; Vylla Poe Watson, "Tree Memorials and the Hall of Fame," *DAR Magazine* 55 (May 1921): 267–73; Prof. Charles Sprague Sargent, "Buckeyes," *Annual Report of the Mount Vernon Ladies' Association of the Union 1917* (Fairfax County, VA): 49; Charles Sprague Sargent, *The Trees at Mount Vernon* (Washington, DC: Reprinted from the Annual Report for 1917 of the Mount Vernon Ladies' Association of the Union), pp. 1, 6 http://babel.hathitrust.org/cgi/pt?id=uc2.ark:/13960/t8sb4690m; Phyllis Andersen, "'If Washington Were Here Himself, He Would Be on My Side': Charles Sprague Sargent and the Preservation of the Mount Vernon Landscape," in *Design with Culture: Claiming America's Landscape Heritage*, eds. Charles A. Birnbaum and Mary V. Hughes (Charlottesville, VA: University of Virginia Press, 2005), pp. 39-56.

6. Howard Mansfield, "The Washington Elm Reassembled," in *The Bones of the Earth* (Washington, DC: Shoemaker Hoard, 2004), pp. 19–34; Samuel F. Batchelder, *The Washington Elm Tradition, "Under this tree Washington first took command of the American Army." Is it true?* (Cambridge, MA: 1925), reprinted from the *Cambridge Tribune*; J. G. Jack, "The Cambridge Washington Elm," *Arnold Arboretum Harvard University Bulletin of Popular Information* 5 (December 10, 1931): 69–73, in acc. file; "Washington Elm Will Be Cut to Bits," *Boston Daily Globe*, October 28, 1923, p. 15; "Guard Washington Elm from Souvenir Hunters," *Boston Daily Globe*, October 29, 1923, p. 5; "Many Ideas as to Washington Elm," *Boston Daily Globe*, October 30, 1923, p. 3; "Hundreds Want Elm Souvenirs," *Boston Daily Globe*, November 1, 1923, p. 8; "Cambridge to Present Flyer a Plane Model Made from Noted Elm," *Boston Daily Globe*, July 21, 1927, p. 22.

CHAPTER THREE

1. "Department of the Fine Arts Report of Archibald Robertson, Esq.," in Cadwallader D. Colden, *Memoir Prepared at the Request of Committee of the Common Council of the City of New York and Presented to the Mayor of the City at the Celebration of the Completion of the New York Canals* (New York: W. A. Davis, 1825), especially pp. 339-341, 346-348; Charles Over Cornelius, *Furniture Masterpieces of Duncan Phyfe* (New York: Metropolitan Museum of Art, 1922), p. 42; Gerald Koeppel,

*Bond of Union: Building the Erie Canal and the American Empire* (Philadelphia, PA: Da Capo, 2009), p. 384.

2. Farwell became a telephone executive and was the president of the Independent Citizens Telephone Company of Terre Haute, Indiana, at the time of his donation (business card in acc. file 68308). For a thumbnail biography, see "Hart F. Farwell, Wabash Valley Profiles," Wabash Valley Visions and Voices, http://visions.indstate.edu/cdm4/item_viewer. php?CISOROOT=/vchs&CISOPTR=527&CISOBOX=1&R EC=4; in 2005 a duplicate gold spike made at the time for the Pacific Railroad came to public attention and is now exhibited by the California State Railroad Museum in Sacramento. The traditional first Golden Spike is displayed in the collection of Stanford University, see California State Railroad Museum, http://www.csrmf.org/events-exhibits/whats-new/see-the-golden-lost-spike-at-the-museum; the extra gold from one of the Pacific Railroad's spikes was turned into miniature spikes for the railroad's directors. Lovett wrote Wolcott that he would be happy to show him his miniature spike when they next met. No donation offer was extended. Charles D. Wolcott to Robert S. Lovett, May 10, 1922, and Lovett to Wolcott, May 19, 1922, acc. file 68308. Lovett enclosed a recent article about the ceremony: C. J. Lane, "Driving the Last Spike," *Union Pacific Magazine* 1 (May 1922): 6, 46; "The Event," *Great Trans-Continental Railroad Guide* (Chicago, IL: Crofutt & Eaton, 1870), pp. 133–34. Another writer estimated that "probably within the first six months there were used as many new ties." Henry T. Williams, *The Pacific Tourist: Williams' Illustrated Trans-Continental Guide of Travel from the Atlantic to the Pacific Ocean* (New York: Henry T. Williams, 1876), p. 166.

3. On Eads's use of "ironclad," see Eads to Fox, September 2, 1872, box 12, folder 10, letters received; in re: Fox's request for a picture of the bridge, Fox to Eads, October 8, 1869, Series X, letterbook 6; Eads to Fox, November 15, 1869, box 12, folder 4, letters received, A–L 1869, Gustava Vasa Fox papers, New-York Historical Society; James B. Eads, *Eads Bridge at St. Louis* (46 leaves of places, n.d.), Smithsonian Institution Libraries collection, features construction diagrams and photographs; John A. Kouwenhoven, "The Designing of the Eads Bridge," *Technology and Culture* 23 (October 1982): 535–68; Howard S. Miller and Quinta Scott, *The Eads Bridge* (Columbia, MO: University of Missouri Press, 1979); Henry Petroski, *Engineers of Dreams: Great Bridge Builders and the Spanning of America* (New York: Alfred A. Knopf, 1995), pp. 22–65; Robert W. Jackson, *Rails Across the Mississippi: A History of the St. Louis Bridge* (Urbana and Chicago: University of Illinois Press, 2001).

4. "Washington's Big Work," *New York Times*, February 23, 1906, p. 7; photograph, "Annual Banquet of the Sons of the Revolution in the State of New York, Delmonico's, Feb. 22, 1906," Library of Congress, http://www.loc.gov/pictures/item/2007663524/; Samuel Y. Edgerton, Jr., "The Franklin Stove," in I. Bernard Cohen, *Benjamin Franklin's Science* (Cambridge, MA: Harvard University Press, 1990), pp. 199–211; Priscilla J. Brewer, *From Fireplace to Cookstove: Technology and the Domestic Ideal in America* (Syracuse, NY: Syracuse University Press, 2000), pp. 28–30; 47–48; Brooke Hindle, *David Rittenhouse* (Princeton, NJ: Princeton University Press, 1964).

5. David P. Billington and Donald C. Jackson, *Big Dams of the New Deal Era: A Confluence of Engineering and Politics* (Norman, OK: University of Oklahoma Press, 2006), pp. 152, 168, 174–92; Paul C. Pitzer, *Grand Coulee: Harnessing a Dream* (Pullman, WA: Washington State University Press, 1994), pp. 78–80; 101–2; 167–71; 248–50; L. Vaughn Downs, *The Mightiest of Them All: Memories of Grand Coulee Dam* (New York: ASCE Press, 1993), p. 71; Harold L. Ickes, *The Secret Diary of Harold L. Ickes* (New York: Simon and Schuster, 1954), 1: 182–84; 2: 494–95; 3: 603–4.

CHAPTER FOUR

1. "Criminal Relics High," *Washington Post*, January 29, 1905, p. E12.

2. Memorandum, Richard H. Howland to Dr. Washburn, November 3, 1964, acc. file 70138, NMAH.

3. Franklin Hunter Churchill, *Sketch of the Life of Bvt. Brig. Gen. Sylvester Churchill, Inspector General U.S. Army* (New York: Willis McDonald, 1888), p. 195; Arthur Lowndes, ed., "William Bayard," in *Archives of the General Convention, Edited by Order of the Commission on Archives Volume III the Correspondence of John Henry Hobart, 1802 to September 1804* (New York: privately printed, 1912), pp. 399–405; Theodore T. Belote to Prof. Holmes, January 5, 1914, acc. file 57108, Office of the Registrar, NMAH.

4. Tammis K. Groft and Mary Alice Mackay, eds., *Albany Institute of History & Art: 200 Years of Collecting* (New York: Hudson Hills Press in association with Albany Institute of History & Art, 1998), p. 279, n. 11; Robert I. Goler, *The Legacy of Lafayette* (New York: Fraunces Tavern Museum, 1984), p. 15; Angus Trumble, *The Finger: A Handbook* (New York: Farrar, Straus and Giroux, 2010), p. 134; Henry Francis du Pont Winterthur Museum, *Lafayette the Nation's Guest: A Picture Book of Mementos which Express the Respect and Affection of the American People for Lafayette* (Winterthur, DE: Henry Francis du Pont Winterthur Museum, 1957), cited in Stephanie Kermes, *Creating an American Identity: New England, 1789–1825* (New York: Palgrave Macmillan, 2008), pp. 119, 250; Edgar Ewing Brandon, comp. and ed., *A Pilgrimage of Liberty: A Contemporary Account of the Triumphal Tour of General Lafayette Through the Southern and Western States in 1825, As Reported by the Local Newspapers* (Athens, OH: Lawhead Press, 1944) and *Lafayette, Guest of the Nation States*, cited in Anne C. Loveland, "Lafayette's Farewell Tour," in Stanley J. Idzerda, Marc H. Miller, and Anne C. Loveland, *Lafayette, Hero of Two Worlds: The Art and Pageantry of His Farewell Tour of America, 1824–1825* (Hanover, NH: distributed by University Press of New England for The Queens Museum of Art, 1989), pp. 63–90; Advertisement, "For Sale at the Haverhill Bookstore," *Haverhill Gazette* (published as *Gazette & Patriot*), September 18, 1824, p. 3.

5. Ben Harris McClary, "Hew Ainslie," American National Biography Online, http://www.anb.org/articles/16/16-00019. html; Hew Ainslie, *Scottish Songs, Ballads, and Poems* (New York: Redfield, 1855), Open Library, http://www.archive. org/stream/scottishsongsbal00ains#page/n7/mode/2up; Clive Wainwright, *The Romantic Interior* (New Haven, CT:

Yale University Press, 1989), pp. 147–207, 151; Mary Monica Maxwell Scott, *Abbotsford: The Personal Relics and Antiquarian Treasures of Sir Walter Scott* (London: Adam and Charles Black, 1893); Jerry E. Patterson, *A Collector's Guide to Relics & Memorabilia* (New York: Crown, 1974), pp. 116–21.

6. The canes and other items are itemized in *Report on the Progress and Condition of the United States National Museum* (Washington, DC: Government Printing Office, 1915), pp. 91, 191; "Homer N. Lockwood Dead," *Washington Post*, June 17, 1913, p. 14; "Willed to City Charities," *New York Times*, September 18, 1913, p. 6.

7. Boehmer's "History of the Smithsonian Exchanges," published in the Secretary's *Reports* for 1881, 1883, and 1887, are summarized in J. H. Kidder, "Report Upon International Exchanges, Under the Direction of the Smithsonian Institution, for the Year Ending June 30, 1888," in *Annual Report of the Board of Regents of the Smithsonian Institution… to July 1888. Appendix III* (Washington, DC: Government Printing Office, 1890), pp. 103–16. On Boehmer's career, see "The U.S. Signal Service Station on the Summit of Pike's Peak," *Harper's Weekly*, November 8, 1873, cited in John Fetler, *The Pikes Peak People: The Story of America's Most Popular Mountain* (Caldwell, ID: Caxton, 1966); Boehmer, "Report on Astronomical Observatories," *Annual Report of the Board of Regents of the Smithsonian Institution… for the Year Ending June 30, 1886. Part I* (Washington, DC: Government Printing Office, 1889), pp. 367–483; Daniel S. Lamb, "The Story of the Anthropological Society of Washington," *American Anthropologist* 8 (1906): 564–79; "Affairs in Washington: A Literary and Scientific Clearing-House," *New York Times*, August 27, 1883, p. 1; "Mr. Boehmer's Mission: What His Trip to Europe for the Smithsonian Accomplished," *Washington Post*, January 31, 1886, p. 4.

8. "Dickens's Sale," *American Literary Gazette and Publisher's Circular* 15–16, August 1, 1870, p. 191; Charles Dickens [*sic*], "Disappearing Dickensland," *North American Review* 156 (June 1893): 670–84; "Wreckers Attack Newgate Prison," *Chicago Daily Tribune*, August 15, 1902, p. 3; "Relics of Newgate Prison," *Law Notes* (September 1902): 110; "Newgate Prison Relics Sold," *New York Times*, February 5, 1903, p. 2; "Criminal Relics High," *Washington Post*, January 29, 1905, p. E12; William J. Carlton, "The Third Man at Newgate," *Review of English Studies* 8 (November 1957): 402–7; Harold D. Kalman, "Newgate Prison," *Architectural History* 12 (1969): 50–112; Billie Melman, *The Culture of History: English Uses of the Past 1800–1953* (New York: Oxford University Press, 2006), pp. 98–101.

9. George Frederick Kunz, American National Biography Online, http://www.anb.org/articles/20/20-00549-print.html; George Frederick Kunz, *The Dedication of the Statue of Joan of Arc in the City of New York on the 6th of December, 1915* (New York: American Scenic and Historic Preservation Society, 1916); "Joan of Arc Statue Dedicated at New York December 6, 1915," acc. file, NMAH; Joan of Arc Statue Committee, *Joan of Arc Loan Exhibition Catalogue* (New York: Joan of Arc Statue Committee, 1913); George Frederick Kunz, "Immunity of Monuments, Museums,

Libraries, Architectural and Historical Structures in War and Peace," *Scientific Monthly* 2 (April 1916): 391–96; James M. Lindgren, "'The Blow Which Civilization Has Suffered': American Preservationists and the Great War, 1914–1919," *Public Historian* 27 (Summer 2005): 27–56; Randall Mason, "Historic Preservation, Public Memory, and the Making of Modern New York City," in *Giving Preservation a History: Histories of Historic Preservation in the United States*, ed. Max Page and Randall Mason (New York: Routledge, 2004), pp. 131–62; Nora M. Heimann, *Joan of Arc: Her Image in France and America* (Washington, DC: Corcoran Gallery of Art in association with D. Giles, 2006); "Big Exhibit in Honor of Joan of Arc's Birthday," *New York Times*, January 5, 1913, p. SM9; "Gather at Shrine of Joan of Arc," *New York Times*, January 7, 1913, p. 7; "French Ruin for Us," *New York Times*, June 14, 1914, p. C2; "Cathedral at Rheims Burned," *Boston Daily Globe*, September 21, 1914, p. 1; "Joan of Arc Statue Unveiled in Drive," *New York Times*, December 7, 1915, p. 13; Records of the American Scenic and Historic Preservation Society, New York Preservation Archive Project, http://www.nypap.org/content/american-scenic-and-historic-preservation-society.

10. "Capt. Allan McLane Dead," *Washington Post*, December 17, 1891, p. 4. "Abby Knight McLane," *New York Times*, March 12, 1919, p. 13.

11. Evelyn Preuss, "The Wall You Will Never Know," Prospects 36 (2005): 19–31; Brian Ladd, *The Ghosts of Berlin: Confronting German History in the Urban Landscape* (Chicago, IL: University of Chicago Press, 1997); John F. Kennedy, "President John F. Kennedy, West Berlin, June 26, 1963, Remarks in the Rudolph Wilde Platz," United States Diplomatic Mission to Germany, http://usa.usembassy.de/etexts/ga5-630626.htm; Ronald Reagan, "Remarks at Brandenberg Gate, Berlin, June 12, 1987," United States Diplomatic Mission to Germany, http://usa.usembassy.de/etexts/ga5-870612.htm; Vladislav M. Zubok, "Khruschev and the Berlin Crisis (1958–1962)," Woodrow Wilson International Center for Scholars: Cold War International History Project, http://www.wilsoncenter.org/sites/default/files/ACFB7D.pdf; Robert D. Schulzinger, "The End of the Cold War, 1961–1991," *OAH Magazine of History* 8 (Winter 1994): 13–18; Walter LaFeber, *America, Russia and the Cold War, 1945–1990* (New York: McGraw-Hill, 1991), pp. 13–22; 38–40; 329–35.

## CHAPTER FIVE

1. Helen Richmond, *Isaac Hull: A Forgotten American Hero* (Boston: USS Constitution Museum, 1983); Tyrone G. Martin, *A Most Fortunate Ship: A Narrative History of Old Ironsides* (Annapolis, MD: Naval Institute Press, 1997), pp. 237–38; Thomas C. Gillmer, *Old Ironsides: The Rise, Decline, and Resurrection of the USS* Constitution (Camden, ME: International Marine, 1993), pp. 91–95.

2. First-person accounts of the invasion of Mexico may be found in *General Scott and His Staff Comprising Memoirs of Generals* (Freeport, NY: Books for Libraries, 1970; first published in 1848). For a map overview of Scott's campaign,

see http://upload.wikimedia.org/wikipedia/commons/6/65/ Mexican_war_overview.gif; "William Henry Browne," in Charles Morris, ed., *Men of the Century: An Historical Work Giving Portraits and Sketches of Eminent Citizens of the United States* (Philadelphia: L. R. Hamersly, 1896), p. 210; William H. Powell, ed., *Officers of the Volunteer Army and Navy who Served in the Civil War* (Philadelphia: L. R. Hamersly, 1893). For Browne's published works, see William Henry Browne, "The Mexican Coquette," in John S. Hart, ed., *The Iris: An Illuminated Souvenir* (Philadelphia: Lippincott, Grambo, 1853), pp. 65–88; Browne, *A Treatise on the Law of Trade-Marks and Anomalous Subjects* (Boston: Little, Brown, 1873). Additional about the war in general: Timothy D. Johnson, *Winfield Scott; The Quest for Military Glory* (Lawrence, KS: University of Kansas Press, 1998), pp. 149–207; Richard Bruce Winders, *Mr. Polk's Army: The American Military Experience in the Mexican War* (College Station, TX: Texas A&M University Press, 1997); K. Jack Bauer, *The Mexican War, 1846–1848* (Lincoln, NE: University of Nebraska Press, 1992); John S. D. Eisenhower, *So Far from God: The U.S. War with Mexico* (New York: Random House, 1989).

3. R. M. Simms, late Captain C.S.A. to J. L. Smith, May 12, 1886, in *Antietam to Appomattox with 118th Penna. Vols., Corn Exchange Regiment. With Descriptions of Marches, Battles and Skirmishes, together with a Complete Roster and Sketches of Officers and Men, compiled from Official Reports, Letters and Diaries* (Philadelphia: J. L. Smith, 1892), pp. 589–91; in 1970 curator Herbert Collins learned from Louis Siebold, grandson of Colonel Whitaker, that he had a portion of the towel with a document signed by Whitaker, and that a portion of the towel was placed in Grant's tomb, accession 124419.

4. Albert E. Johnson, "Reminiscences of the Hon. Edwin M. Stanton, Secretary of War," *Records of the Columbian Historical Society, Washington, DC* 13 (1913): 69–97; *Richmond Whig*, April 27–28, 1865. Special thanks to Nancy Bercaw who called my attention to this quote.

5. *The Century Magazine* published firsthand accounts of the surrender, including General Horace Porter, "Campaigning with Grant," *The Century Illustrated Monthly Magazine*, October 1897, pp, 879–98, which describes the chairs, the table, and the role of Colonel Charles Marshall as Lee's military secretary, p. 881; Colonel Charles Marshall, "The Last Days of Lee's Army," *The Century Illustrated Monthly Magazine*, April 1902, pp. 932–35, describes the table's use by Grant's military secretary Colonel Ely S. Parker, p. 934; E. P. Alexander, "Lee at Appomattox: Personal Recollections of the Break-Up of the Confederacy," *The Century Illustrated Monthly Magazine*, April 1902, pp. 921–31, describes Alexander's encounter with an addled Wilmer McLean, p. 931. General Porter's account was later compiled in Porter, *Campaigning with Grant* (New York: Da Capo Press, 1897, 1986), pp. 471–84. Ulysses S. Grant described the surrender without reference to relics, U. S. Grant, *Personal Memoirs of U. S. Grant* (New York: Charles L. Webster, 1886), pp. 486–98. For Blackmar's display of the Grant chair, see "By His Comrades. Reception to Gen. W. W. Blackmar, Department Commander of the Massachusetts G.A.R.," *Boston Daily Globe*, March 29, 1902,

p. 3. A useful secondary account of the surrender at the McLean house is Lucille McWane Watson, "Lee and Grant Return to Appomattox," *The Iron Worker* 19 (Spring 1955): 1–14, found with related correspondence and undated newspaper clippings in acc. file 45493, NMAH.

6. "Peace Treaty Souvenirs," *Boston Daily Globe*, November 11, 1914, p. 4; "Paperweight Souvenir Explained in a Letter from William J. Bryan," *Atlanta Constitution*, January 20, 1917, p. 6; "Rule or Ruin, Bryan's Policy at the Frisco Convention," *Washington Post*, May 9, 1920, p. 27.

7. Lewis L. Strauss, *Men and Decision* (New York: Macmillan, 1962), p. 42; Herbert Hoover, *The Memoirs of Herbert Hoover: Years of Adventure, 1874–1920* (New York: Macmillan, 1951), pp. 345–46; George H. Nash, *The Life of Herbert Hoover: Master of Emergencies 1917–1918* (New York: W. W. Norton, 1996), 2: 30, 66; Harry R. Rudin, *Armistice 1918* (New Haven, CT: Yale University Press, 1944); "Lewis L. Strauss, Ex-AEC Chairman, Dies at Age 77," *Washington Post*, January 22, 1974, p. C9; "Lewis Strauss Dies; Ex-Head of A.E.C.," *New York Times*, January 22, 1974, p. S1.

CHAPTER SIX

1. James Parton, *Life of Andrew Jackson* (New York: Mason Brothers, 1860), 1: 104–5; Jethro Rumple, *A History of Rowan County, North Carolina* (Westminster, MD: Heritage, 1916; reprint 2005), pp. 194, 198–99; for the ongoing search for the building, see Mark Wineka, "Location of Historic Salisbury Law Office Still a Mystery," *Salisbury Post*, May 27, 2005.

2. Fred Sumner, "Nashville Tenn 7th Feby 1845," object documentation file, cat. 227739.1845.X1, Division of Political History, NMAH; "From the Globe. Mr. Van Buren's Visit to the Hermitage," *Ohio Statesman* (Columbus, Ohio), May 18, 1842, p. 2. Thanks to Marsha Mullin for calling my attention to this quote.

3. Entry for September 25, 1855, Varden diaries, SIA.

4. Wayne C. Temple, "Lincoln's Fence Rails," *Journal of the Illinois State Historical Society* 47 (Spring 1954): 20–34; James T. Hickey, "Oglesby's Fence Rail Dealings and the 1860 Decatur Convention," *Journal of the Illinois State Historical Society* 54 (Spring 1961): 5–24; Mark A. Plummer, Richard J. Oglesby, "Lincoln's Rail-Splitter," *Illinois Historical Journal* 80 (Spring 1987): 2–12. After Chicago, Dennis Hanks and John Hanks erected the cabin on Boston Common, where they sold souvenirs. William E. Barton, *Additional Information: The Lincoln Cabin on Boston Common* (Peoria, IL: E. J. Jacob, 1929). On the Chicago fairs in the context of the sanitary-fair movement, see Gordon, *Bazaars and Fair Ladies*, pp. 58–93.

5. Jessie Fant Evans, "Lincoln's Blood Stains Cuff Owned by Mrs. S. P. Thompson," Washington *Star*, February 7, 1937 (newspaper clipping in acc. file); Terry Theodore, "Laura Keene and Mr. Lincoln," *Lincoln Herald* 73 (1971): 199–204; Billy J. Harbin, "Laura Keene at the Lincoln Assassination," *Educational Theatre Journal* 18 (March 1966): 47–54; Michael W. Kauffman, *American Brutus: John Wilkes Booth and the Lincoln Conspiracies* (New York: Random House, 2004), pp, 4–18, 36; Vernanne Bryan, *Laura Keene: A British*

Actress on the American Stage, 1826–1873 (Jefferson, NC: McFarland, 1997); Alan S. Downer, ed., *The Autobiography of Joseph Jefferson* (Cambridge, MA: Belknap Press of Harvard University Press, 1964), pp. 139–56. Ben Graf Henneke, *Laura Keene: A Biography* (Tulsa, OK: Council Oaks, 1990) acknowledges the cuff (p. 293) and the legacy of Keene's dress, which was cut up into panels by Keene's granddaughter and distributed to friends around 1890 (pp. 218–19); Dorothy Meserve Kunhardt and Philip B. Kunhardt, Jr., *Twenty Days* (New York: Castle, 1965); Timothy S. Good, *We Saw Lincoln Shot: One Hundred Eye Witness Accounts* (Jackson, MI: University Press of Mississippi, 1995), pp. 22-24; 103-104.

6. Wedgwood miniatures including a similar creamer are pictured in Harry M. Buten, *Wedgwood ABC—But Not Middle E* (Merion, PA: Buten Museum of Wedgwood, 1964), p. 80.

7. "Relic Hunters Haunt the White House," *New York Times*, June 23, 1902, p. 3; "Vandals Barred at White House," *Chicago Daily Tribune*, July 14, 1902, p. 2; "What Becomes of the Relics!" *Chicago Daily Tribune*, July 17, 1902, p. 12.

8. "A Brief Account of the Smithsonian African Expedition," n.d., acc. file 259674; Theodore Roosevelt, *African Game Trails: An Account of the African Wanderings of an American Hunter-Naturalist* (New York: Scribner, 1910), p. 27; Kermit Roosevelt, *The Happy Hunting Grounds* (New York: Scribner, 1920), pp. 23–24; R. L. Wilson, *Theodore Roosevelt: Outdoorsman* (New York: Winchester, 1976), pp. 172–202; Edmund Morris, *Colonel Roosevelt* (New York: Random House, 2010), pp. 3–26.

9. Robert Trout, "The First Fireside Chat," typescript, n.d., acc. file; Russell D. Buhite and David W. Levy, eds., *FDR's Fireside Chats* (Norman, OK: University of Oklahoma Press, 1992); Samuel I. Rosenman, *Working with Roosevelt* (New York: Harper, 1952), pp. 39, 92–97; William L. Bird, Jr., *"Better Living": Advertising, Media, and the New Vocabulary of Business Leadership, 1935–1955* (Evanston, IL: Northwestern University Press, 1999), pp. 10–12; David Halberstam, *The Powers That Be* (New York: Knopf, 1975), pp. 12–18. On the papers' retouching of negatives, see O. B. Hanson to H. C. Luttgens, "Microphones and Name Plates—NBC Microphones at World's Fair," June 2, 1933, box 16: NBC Central Files correspondence, folder 46: Century of Progress— Chicago World's Fair 1933, National Broadcasting Company collection, State Historical Society of Wisconsin.

10. David M. Oshinsky, *Polio: An American Story* (New York: Oxford University Press, 2005), pp. 24–53; Richard Thayer Goldberg, *The Making of Franklin D. Roosevelt: Triumph Over Disability* (Cambridge, MA: Abt, 1981), pp. 151–60; "Capital Leads Nation Feting Roosevelt, 52," *New York*

*Times*, January 31, 1934, pp. 1, 4; Scott M. Cutlip, *Fundraising in the United States: Its role in America's Philanthropy* (New Brunswick, NJ: Rutgers University Press, 1965), pp. 364-82.

11. "New 'Necktie Poll' Puts Dewey Ahead Despite 'Tie' Vote," *Nashville Banner*, October 22, 1948, p. 9; Zachary Karabell, *The Last Campaign: How Harry Truman Won the 1948 Election* (New York: Knopf, 2001), pp. 93–94, 186, 200, 255–57; Gary A. Donaldson, *Truman Defeats Dewey* (Lexington, KY: University Press of Kentucky, 1999), pp. 209–14; Harold I. Gulian, *The Upset that Wasn't: Harry S. Truman and the Crucial Election of 1948* (Chicago: Ivan R. Dee, 1998); Richard Norton Smith, *Thomas E. Dewey and His Times* (New York: Simon and Schuster, 1984); George H. Gallup, oral history interview transcript, 1972, Columbia University Oral History Office, New York, NY; James Playsted Wood, "George H. Gallup," *Journal of Marketing* 26 (October 1962): 78–80.

12. Edith P. Mayo, "Be a Party Girl: Campaign Appeal to Women," in Keith E. Melder, *Hail to the Candidate: Presidential Campaigns from Banners to Broadcasts* (Washington, DC: Smithsonian Institution Press, 1992), pp. 149–60.

13. Frank Stanton to S. Dillon Ripley, March 14, 1977, acc. file; Holcomb B. Noble, "Frank Stanton, Broadcast Pioneer, Dies at 98," *New York Times*, December 25, 2006, pp. A1, B7.

14. John Hersey, "Survival," New Yorker, June 17, 1944, 31–34+; *Readers Digest* 45 (August 1944): 75–80; William Safire describes the tie clasp as "the highest status symbol of the New Frontier": "Cufflinks Gang," in Safire, *Safire's Political Dictionary* (New York: Oxford University Press, 1978), pp. 159–60. Lincoln's association with Kennedy is described in Evelyn Lincoln, *My Twelve Years with John F. Kennedy* (New York: D. McKay, 1965). A "group of eleven tie clasps and twelve pins in plastic boxes" belonging to Jacqueline Kennedy were relinquished by Caroline and John Kennedy in 1995 to the Kennedy Library. Deborah Mitchell, "Jackie's Things," and "What Caroline Kennedy and JFK Jr. Gave Up," New York, July 31, 1995, 20–21; David Samuels, "Going, Going…A sale of John F. Kennedy's effects raises the question: Who owns J.F.K.?" *New Yorker*, January 19, 1998, 27–28; Robert M. Adler, "The Public Controversy Over the Kennedy Memorabilia Project," in Francis X. Blouin, Jr., and William G. Rosenberg, eds., *Archives, Documentation, and Institutions of Social Memory: Essays from the Sawyer Seminar* (Ann Arbor: University of Michigan Press, 2006), pp. 225–36.

15. Larry Bird, "Eyeballing the Vote," *Smithsonian*, October 2004, pp. 45–46.

# CREDITS

INTRODUCTION

**Fig. 1:** James Smithson's carte de visite, ca. 1826. 3" x 1 ⅝", cat. 2011.0013.02. Front: AHB #2012q08025; reverse (with inscription): AHB #2012q08038.

**Fig. 2:** George Washington button and handwritten museum label. Button: 1 ⅜" diam. x ⅛", acc. 13152, cat. 16162, SI #2012-04314; label: 3 ⅜" x 3", AHB #2012q08026.

**Fig. 3:** Lock of President Rutherford B. Hayes's hair with White House envelope, 1884. Envelope: 6" x 3 ⅜", acc. 14161, cat. 75013, SI #RWS2012-04289.

**Fig. 4:** Thomas Jefferson desk and note. Desk (closed): 14 ⅜" x 9 ¾" x 3 ¼", acc. 67435, cat. 31819, SI #ET2012-12442; note: 8" x 7". Transcription: Th. Jefferson gives this Writing Desk to Joseph Coolidge, Jr. as a memorial of affection. It was made from a drawing of his own, by Ben. Randall, cabinet maker of Philadelphia, with whom he first lodged on his arrival in that city in May 1776 and is the identical one on which he wrote the Declaration of Independence. Politics as well as Religion has its superstitions. These, gaining strength with time, may, one day, give imaginary value to this relic, for its association with the birth of the Great Charter of our Independence. Monticello, Nov. 18, 1825.

**Fig. 5:** George Washington embossed postcard, Germany, circa 1906. 6" x 3 ⅜", acc. 227739.1789.S4, AHB #2012q08028.

**Fig. 6:** Photograph of John Varden. Copy photograph, AHB #2012q08029.

**Fig. 7:** George Washington's coach panel. Panel: 17" x 15" x 2", acc. 13152, cat. 16107, SI #2012-04585; label: 4 ⅞" x 3 ½", AHB #2012q08030.

**Fig. 8:** Photograph of George Washington relics displayed at the 1876 centennial celebration. Copy photograph: SI #74-388-35.

**Fig. 9:** Photograph of *History of the United States* exhibit, North Hall, USNM, circa 1904. Glass-plate negative, SI #16241.

**Fig. 10:** Group of McKinley and Bryan pin-back buttons. Gift of Paul Beckwith, acc. 37407, SI #RWS2012-04586.

**Fig. 11:** Photograph of DAR case, North Hall, USNM. Cyanotype, AHB#2012q080044; scan of original glass-plate negative, SI #14414.

**Fig. 12:** Photograph of index exhibit, *History: The Record of Events and Personalities*, Smithsonian Castle, 1941. Scan of negative, SI #34545.

THE SOUVENIRS

**I. The Cause of Freedom**

**p. 48:** Plymouth Rock fragment, Plymouth, Massachusetts, 1830. 2 ¾" x 4 ¼" x ⅞", acc. 52309, cat. 12058, SI RWS2012-04276.

**p. 50:** Oak cane made from an original floor joist of Independence Hall, Philadelphia, Pennsylvania, 1873. 34 ½" x 1"diam., acc. 99344, cat. 35668, SI #2012-04345.

**p. 52:** Wooden nutmeg and unfinished wood from the Connecticut Charter Oak, Hartford, Connecticut, 1856–1881. Nutmeg: 2 ⅝" x 2 ⅛" diam., acc. 26480, cat. 6186; unfinished piece: 20" x 7" x 4", acc. 55163, cat. 14132, SI #RWS2012-05620; trade card: 5 ⅜" x ⅜", AHB #2012q08034.

**p. 54:** Souvenir Statue of Liberty, New York, New York, 1885. 6" x 1 ⅝" x 1 ½", acc. 16237, cat. 1650, SI #RWS2012-04272.

**p. 56:** "Jailed for Freedom" suffrage pin, Washington, DC, 1917. 1 ½" x 1" x ¼", cat. 229385.03, SI #RWS2012-05663.

**II. The Immortal Washington**

**p. 60:** Piece of George Washington's mahogany coffin with note, Mount Vernon, Virginia, circa 1840. 1 ⅞" x 2¼" x ¾", cat. 2011.0013.02, SI #RWS2012-04283.

ACCESSION. 26480

002

THIS IS TO CERTIFY that this Wooden Nutmeg was made from the Original Charter Oak Tree, from pieces saved by Robbins & Winship when they made the Governor s Chair which is now in the State Capitol at Hartford, Conn.

Mr. Winship was my father-in-law.

Company D,
2d Connecticut
Heavy Artillery.

W. H WHITELAW,
104 CAPITOL AV

Return to Registrar.

**LEFT**

Affidavit, Charter Oak nutmeg, p.52

**p. 62:** Wooden George Washington plaque from James Crutchett's Mount Vernon Factory, Washington, DC, 1859. Front: 3 ⅛" diam. x ⅜", cat. 2011.0013.01, SI #RWS2012-04342; reverse: AHB #2012q08043.

**p. 64:** Old ivy from Mount Vernon, Mount Vernon, Virginia, 1879. 1 ½" x ⅝" x ⅜", acc. 49603, cat. 11196, SI #RWS2012-05632.

**p. 66:** Washington Monument cornerstone piece, Washington, DC, 1880. 4 ¾" x 4 ½" x 1", cat. 235052.01, SI #RWS2012-04275.

**p. 68:** Brick collected at Wakefield, George Washington's boyhood home, Westmoreland County, Virginia, 1894. 7" x 5" x 3" acc. 32247, cat. 202319, SI #RWS2012-05628.

**p. 70:** Miniature compass embedded in a nut from Mount Vernon, Mount Vernon, Virginia, undated. 1" x ⅝" x ⅜", cat. 234919.01, SI #RWS2012-05621.

**p. 72:** Wooden compotes made from the Washington Elm, Cambridge, Massachusetts, 1924. 4 ⅛" x 2 ⅞" diam. x 2 ⅜" diam., cat. 320013.01; 4 ½" x 3 ¼" diam. x 1 ½" diam., cat. 230013.02, SI #RWS2012-04587.

### III. Industrial Revolutions

**p. 76:** Medal box made from wood carried on the *Seneca Chief*, opening of the Erie Canal, Erie, Pennsylvania, 1825. 2" diam. x ½", cat. 2011.0036.07, SI #RWS2012-04284.

**p. 78:** Wooden chip cut from a railroad tie, Promontory, Utah, 1869. 1 ⅜" x ⅝" x ⅛", acc. 68308, cat. 32197, SI #RWS2012-05635.

**p. 80:** Piece of Mississippi bedrock from beneath the east pier of the St. Louis (Eads) Bridge, St. Louis, Missouri, 1871–1874.

Bedrock: 2 ¾" x 1 ½" x ¾", acc. 52309, cat. 12059, SI #2012-04273; drawing: 21 ¾" x 5", acc. 52309, cat. 12059, AHB #2012q08035.

**p. 82:** Miniature copper model of the Franklin Stove, New York, New York, 1906. 4 ¼" x 3 ¼" x 2 ⅝", acc. 46834, cat. 10788, SI #RWS2012-05630.

**p. 84:** Letter opener made from a shovel used in building the Grand Coulee Dam, Spokane, Washington, 1933–1942. 10 ⅛" x 1 ¼" x ½", cat. 1977.0783.05, SI #RWS2012-05623.

### IV. Foreign Guests

**p. 88:** Piece of the Bastille, Paris, France, 1789. ⁷⁄₁₆" x ⁷⁄₁₆" x ⁵⁄₁₆", acc. 71118, cat. 34262, SI #RWS2012-04280.

**p. 90:** Napoleon's napkin, Island of Elba, Italy, 1815. 35" x 45", acc. 57108, cat. 15037, SI #RWS2012-04326.

**p. 92:** Lady's glove with a portrait of Lafayette, 1824–25. 9" x 3 ½", acc. 54393, cat. 273187, SI #RWS2012-05629.

**p. 94:** Lock of Sir Walter Scott's hair in a glass vial, Melrose, Scotland, 1832. 4" x 4 ⅛" x ½", acc. 11743, cat. 1074, SI #RWS2012-03540.

**p. 96:** Punch marks of the railroad conductors of the world, ca. 1870–1913, acc. 56368. Lockwood explanation: 5" x 2 ½", cat. 14507; Chinese: 5 ⅜" x 3 ⅛", cat. 14508. Sanford Dole: 5 ⅜" x 3 ⅛", cat. 14509; Harrison and Diaz: 4 ½" x 2 ⅜", cat. 14511; case 5 ¼" x 3 ½", SI #RWS2012-04349.

**p. 98:** Piece of mosaic pavement from the palace of Tiberius, Rome, Italy, 1884. ⅞" x ½" x ⅜", acc. 17178, cat. 1700, SI #RWS2012-04291.

**p. 100:** Section of oak beam from the Newgate Prison Chapel, London, England, 1903. 8 ½" x 5" x 5", acc. 44395, cat. 10398, SI #RWS2012-05627; letter: 13" x 8", AHB #2012q08037. Transcription: St. Louis / Bow Street / London, H.C. / England. / to the Secretary of the Smithsonian Institute, / Washington, D.C. / Dear Sir, / This is a section of an "Oak-beam," taken from the Chapel of Newgate Goal, London, England, in the course of demolition 1903, which was burnt by the Gordon Rioters— June, 1780, / vide Barnaby Rudge / By Charles Dickens. / Should you accept this relic into your institution, would you be so kind as to forward me an official receipt to address in London. / I remain / Respectfully yours / William Fulcher. / Police Constable, 259 E. Division / Metropolitan Police Force / London.

**p. 102:** Stone from the dungeon of Joan of Arc, Rouen, France, 1915. Stone: 3 ¾" x 3 ⅝" x 1", acc. 59181, cat. 15842, SI #2012-04588; photograph: Underwood & Underwood, AHB #2012-08044.

**p. 104:** Souvenirs from the cabinet of Abby Knight McLane, Washington, DC, 1919, acc. 63786. Antediluvian oak: 2 ⅝" x 1" x ¼", cat. 33956; stone from Pompeii: ⅜" x ⅜" x ¼", cat. 33954; round metal piece of the HMS *Great Britain*: ⅜" x 1" diam., cat. 33957; piece of cedar door post: 1 ¼" x 1" x 1 ¼", cat. 33951; stone in the shape of an arrowhead: 3 ¼" x 2 ⅝" x ⅜"; cat. 33953, SI #RWS2012-05622.

**p. 106:** Concrete fragment of the Berlin Wall, Berlin, Germany, 1989. 3 ¾" x 3 ¾" x ¾", cat. 2011.0015.01, SI #RWS2012-04341.

UNVEILING THE STATUE OF JOAN OF ARC AT NEW YORK, DECEMBER 6, 1915.  (Smoke from Artillery salute in upper left hand corner.)
(Copyright by Underwood & Underwood, N. Y.)

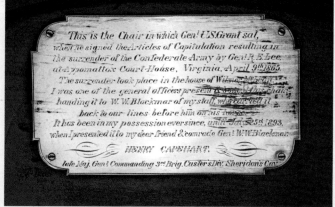

**TOP**

Dedication of the Joan of Arc statue. The dungeon stones make up the six panels set into the sides and on the east (left) end of the pedestal, p. 102

**RIGHT**

Silver provenance plaque attached to the chair in which General U. S. Grant sat at Appomattox, p. 116

**V. Diplomacy and War**

**p. 110:** Vase made from a timber of the USS *Constitution*, Boston, Massachusetts, 1835. 8 ½" diam. x 17", cat. 1994.0207.01, SI #RWS2012-04336.

**p. 112:** Mexican-American War spoils, Amozoc de Mota, Mexico, 1847, acc. 6922. Carved wooden cross: 4 ½" x 2 ½" x ½", cat. 549; rosary: 23 ¼" x 2 ¼" x ½", cat. 549; prayer book: *Meditaciones*: 3" x 2" x ½", cat. 996; embroidered rose on paper: 3 ⅝" x 2 ¾"; cat. 549; beadwork on linen: 8 ¼" x 4 ⅜", cat. 549; checkerboard paper: 3 ⅛" x 3", cat. 549, miniature basket (child's toy): 1 ½" diam. x ¼", cat. 994, SI #RWS2012-05625.

**p. 114:** Towel used as a flag of truce, Appomattox Court House, Virginia, 1865. Towel: 18 ½" x 16", acc. 54044, cat. 272728; letter: 8" x 5", acc. 124419, cat. 39766, SI #RWS2012-04323. Transcription: Head Qrs. 3rd Cav, Div. / Appomattox C. H. Va. / April 10, 1865. / I hereby certify on honor that this towel is the truce used by Capt. Simms [*sic*] of General Longstreet's staff bearing message to Gen. Custer asking cessation of hostilities and to arrest the charge the 3rd Cav. Divn was in the act of making on the center of Lee's Army at 9 A.M. yesterday. This truce was sent out under the direction of Gen. Lee himself and is the first and only one used asking immediate cessation of hostilities that a conference might be held with Gen. Grant who arrived on the field many hours later. / E. W. Whitaker / Lt. Col. 1st Cav.

**p. 116:** Table and chairs used by Robert E. Lee and Ulysses S. Grant, Appomattox Court House, Virginia, 1865. Lee's caned maple armchair: 45 ½" x 18 ½" x 20", acc. 59140, cat. 15829. Pine-top table: 32" x 20" x 27", acc. 124419, cat. 39767; Grant's leather-covered office chair on casters with silver plaque, 38" x 24" x 20", acc. 45493, cat. 10517. Transcription of plaque: This is the Chair in which Genl U.S. Grant sat, / when he signed the Articles of Capitulation resulting in / the surrender of the Confederate Army by Genl R. E. Lee, / at Appomattox Court House, Virginia, April 9th 1865. / The surrender took place in the house of Wilmer McLean. / I was one of the general officers present & bought this chair, / handing it to W. W. Blackmar of my staff, who carried it / back to our lines before him on his horse. / It has been in my possession ever since, until July 25, 1893, / when I presented it

to my dear friend & comrade Genl W. W. Blackmar. / Henry Capehart / late Maj. Genl Commanding 3rd Brig. Custer's Div. Sheridan's Cav. SI #95-5515.

**p. 118:** Punch bowl, executive mansion of the Confederacy, Richmond, Virginia, 1865. 9" x 18" diam., cat. 1984.0623.04, SI #2012-04330.

**p. 120:** "Swords into Plowshares" paperweight designed by William Jennings Bryan, Washington, DC, 1915. 5" x 3 ¼" x 3", cat. 243594.92, SI #RWS2012-04297.

**p. 122:** Fountain pen used to sign the final armistice agreement for the First World War, Brussels, Belgium, 1919. Pen: 6 ⅝" x ⅝" diam., cat. 1979.0657.10; note: 5 ⅝" x 3 ⅝", SI #RWS2012-04295.

**VI. Presidential Pieces**

**p. 126:** Wooden chip from the building in which Andrew Jackson studied law, Salisbury, North Carolina, 1774. 2 ⅝" x ¼", acc. 6922, cat. 549, SI #RWS2012-04595.

**p. 128:** Framed lock of Andrew Jackson's hair with note, near Nashville, Tennessee, 1845. Hair: 4 ⅛" x 4" x ½", cat. 227739. 1845.X1, SI #RWS2012-04288; note: 7 ⅞" x 6 ⅛", AHB #2012q08039. Transcription: Nashville Tenn 7th Feby 1845 / On Friday 7th February 1845 – I left Nashville in Company of / Colonel William H Polk brother to James K Polk President / Just elected of the United States at 9 in the morning on / a visit to the Hermitage which is 12 miles off, arrived / there at half past eleven and found the General in / his bed room, he was sitting in a large chair and / although weak appeared doing pretty well, he told / us he was strong enough to walk about, but did not / do it on account of the difficulty of breathing, he / complains of a pain on the left side and did not / expect to live long he gave me _____ / _____ a / lock of his hair that he cut before us for my / wife and a letter to the President. / Fred Sumner.

**p. 130:** *Hair of Persons of Distinction* and *Hair of the Presidents*, Washington, DC, 1853 and 1855. *Hair of Persons of Distinction*: 18 ½" x 13" x 1", acc. 13152, cat. 16157A, SI #RWS2012-04322; *Hair of the Presidents*: 22 ¼" x 16" x 1", acc. 13152, cat. 16157, SI #RWS2012-04320. Transcription of inscription on reverse of *Hair of Persons of Distinction*: Hair of Presidents of the United States with other Persons of Distinction, / Prepared and arranged by John Varden, February, 1853. / N.B. Those having hair of

Distinguished Persons, / will confere a Favor by adding to this Collection.

**p. 132:** Fence rail split by Abraham Lincoln and John Hanks, Decatur, Illinois, with Hanks's affidavit, 1865. 9" x 3 ½" x 3 ½", cat. 1983.0418.01, SI #RWS2012-04347.

**p. 134:** Laura Keene's bloodstained cuff, worn at Ford's Theater, Washington, DC, 1865. 9" x 3", cat. 242707.01, SI #RWS2012-05626.

**p. 136:** Miniature Wedgwood creamer from the White House, Washington, DC, circa 1897. 2" x 1" diam. x 1", cat. 288940.01, SI #RWS2012-05631.

**p. 138:** Piece of a stud with a nail from the East Room of the White House, Washington, DC, 1902. 6 ⅝" x 2 ⅝" x 4 ¾", cat. 2011.0036.05, SI #RWS2012-04339.

**p. 140:** Fish-shaped can opener used on Theodore Roosevelt's African expedition, 1909–1910, 5" x 1 ¼" x ¾", acc. 259674, cat. 51304, SI #RWS2012-04593.

**p. 142:** Franklin D. Roosevelt's "fireside chat" microphones, Washington, DC, 1933 and 1941. CBS: 8 ½" x 5 ¼" x 4 ¾", cat. 233610.01; NBC: 10 ¼" x 5 ⅞" diam., cat. 1996.0168.01, SI #RWS2012-04317.

**p. 144:** Cake pieces from Franklin D. Roosevelt's birthday ball, Washington, DC, 1934. Each box (closed): 2 ⅝" x 2 ⅝" x 1 ⅛", cat. 1984.0054.01, SI #RWS2012-05624.

**p. 146:** Photograph, Dewey-Truman necktie poll, Harvey's department store, Nashville, Tennessee, 1948. 8" x 10" print from negative, cat. 227739.1948.A8, AHB #2012q08040.

**p. 148:** Bucket used to clean blackboard tallies of election returns, New York, New York, 1952. 10 ½" x (top) 12" diam., (bottom) 8 ⅝" diam., cat. 227739.1952.X29, SI #RWS2012-04334.

**p. 150:** Kennedy-Nixon television debate chairs, Chicago, Illinois, 1960. Each chair: 24 ⅜" x 20 ½" x 29 ⅝", cat. 1977.0541.01-.02, SI #RWS2012-04327. Copy photograph, AHB #2012q08042. Kennedy chair plaque: SI #RWS2012-04329; Nixon chair plaque: SI #RWS 2012-04328.

**p. 152:** Kennedy PT-109 tie clip, Washington, DC, 1960–1963. 1 ¾" x ⅜" x ⅝", cat. 254858.02. SI #RWS2012-04290.

**p. 154:** Magnifying glass and chads, Broward County, Florida, 2000. Magnifying glass: 9 ⅛" x 4 ⅜" x ¾", cat. 2001.0092.03; chads: 4" x 2" x ⅛", cat. 2001.0304.01, SI #RWS2012-04298; Judge Robert Rosenberg. Associated Press photograph by Alan Diaz, #00112402089.

Nashville June 7th Feby 1845

on Friday [of] Februry 1845 I left Nashville in Company of
Colonel William H Polk brother to James K Polk President
just elected of the United States, at 9 in the morning on
a visit to the Hermitage, which is 12 miles off, arrived
there at half past eleven and found the General in
his bed room, he was seating in a large chair and
although weak appeared doing pretty well; he told
us he was strong enough to walk about, but did not
do it on account of the difficulty of breathing; he
complains of a pain on his left side and did not
expect to live long; he gave me on parting a
lock of his hair that he cut before us for my
wife and a letter to the President.

Fred Sumner

**ABOVE**

Fred Sumner's manuscript account
of a visit with Andrew Jackson, in
which Jackson cut a lock of his hair
for Sumner's wife, p. 128

SENATOR JOHN F. KENNEDY
USED THIS CHAIR IN
THE FIRST FACE-TO-FACE DISCUSSION
BETWEEN PRESIDENTIAL CANDIDATES
BROADCAST SEPTEMBER 26, 1960
FROM CBS TELEVISION STUDIO 1
CHICAGO

VICE PRESIDENT RICHARD M. NIXON
USED THIS CHAIR IN
THE FIRST FACE-TO-FACE DISCUSSION
BETWEEN PRESIDENTIAL CANDIDATES
BROADCAST SEPTEMBER 26, 1960
FROM CBS TELEVISION STUDIO 1
CHICAGO

### TOP, LEFT

Moderator Howard K. Smith,
Senator John F. Kennedy, and
Vice-President Richard M. Nixon
on the set of the first televised
presidential debate, Chicago,
Illinois, September 26, 1960

### TOP, RIGHT

Judge Robert Rosenberg
examines a punch-card ballot
during the Broward County,
Florida, presidential-election
recount, 2000, p. 154

### LEFT

Silver provenance plaques
attached to the back of each chair
used by the candidates, p. 150

## About the Author

William L. Bird, Jr., is a historian and curator at the
National Museum of American History, Smithsonian
Institution. He is the author of *America's Doll House, Holidays
on Display*, and *Paint by Number* and coauthor with Harry
Rubenstein of *Design for Victory*. The pictured artifacts are
a Bayeux Tapestry mug purchased by Bird's grandmother while
visiting the British Museum as a young girl and a souvenir
from a construction site near her home in Washington, DC,
collected by Bird himself, which she kept with the mug.

★ ★ ★